CONTENTS

INTRODUCTION

Synopsis: This book presents a novel perspective, with the author analyzing the shortcomings of the Chinese writing system from an economic standpoint. The analysis extends to the resulting adverse phenomena in various areas such as socio-economics, culture, politics, and technology. From the vantage point of historical development, the author proposes a preliminary framework for solutions, aimed at fostering discussion and exchange among those deeply concerned with the fate of the Chinese nation. Additionally, the book explores several other intriguing topics.

Preface

Over the past forty years of reform and opening up, China has experienced continuous economic development and improvement in material living standards. However, its contributions to the world in the fields of culture, arts, and scientific achievements have been underwhelming. Additionally, the country ranks among the highest in the world for the incidence and proportion of depression, schizophrenia, and cancer. As a nation that has essentially modernized and strives to learn from the advanced science and culture of the West in all aspects of social life, what factors have led to these persistent, unresolved issues?

By comparing the civilization of China with those of other countries, we find that apart from unchangeable factors like ethnicity and natural geographic environment, the reasons may lie within the unique aspects of Chinese national culture. The language and writing system, as the carriers of national culture, might be the root cause. Through personal experiences and long-term reflection and verification, I have arrived at some systematic and universal viewpoints. Starting from the analysis of the shortcomings of the Chinese language, I have extended the discussion to various aspects of the spiritual life of the Chinese people. There are no strict limitations on the scope of this analysis, but all topics are closely related to Chinese culture, especially the Chinese language environment.

Given the author's limited research conditions and capabilities, it has been challenging to obtain relevant statistical data. Additionally, the humanities are inherently imprecise disciplines, so these theories cannot be guaranteed to be universally applicable like mathematical formulas. The author aims to provide some interesting and worthwhile research topics as a reference to stimulate thought and discussion. If these ideas can inspire colleagues to propose reasonable solutions, improve the mental well-being of the Chinese people, and accelerate cultural progress, it would be highly beneficial. Should there be any inaccuracies, I welcome corrections from more knowledgeable individuals.

Ⅰ. The Drawbacks of the Chinese Language

Many countries now envy the achievements of China's economic development. Some countries are even preparing to enhance the study and application of the Chinese language. But what is the actual situation with the Chinese language? What problems does it have? After deep reflection, I believe the following points need to be carefully discussed and analyzed.

1. The Fundamental Purpose of Language

The emergence of human civilization can be traced back to the use of pictures. Before writing was invented, humans relied on drawings to record information. At that time, humans likely already had spoken language but no medium for recording it. Clearly, pictorial representation was time-consuming, labor-intensive, and imprecise in conveying meaning. How could we improve the efficiency of information transmission? Ingenious individuals then invented the earliest pictographic characters, which were essentially simplified and condensed versions of pictures. Throughout production practices, humans continually created and improved methods of information expression, eventually forming a standardized linear writing system, which was similar worldwide regardless of the shape of the characters. Functionally, written language serves to disseminate information, including knowledge summarized by predecessors, various true or fictional stories, and abstract concepts that transcend immediate reality, regardless of their value ranking.

So, what problems do pictographic characters have? The issues are quite severe. Looking at some photos of the ancient Mayan civilization, their writing system was pictographic. Each character was a small picture, very complex and difficult to memorize accurately, making writing challenging. Pictographs lack accurate phonetic representation; the pronunciation was transmitted orally. Pronunciation is a crucial tool for human thought. Without the accurate expression of these "sounds" in the brain, information cannot be accurately conveyed, and deeper logical thinking is impeded.

Ironically, due to my limited proficiency in foreign languages, I cannot express these ideas in phonetic languages like English or Japanese. Therefore, this text uses the improved version of ancient pictographic Chinese—Simplified Chinese characters. Chinese characters have evolved from oracle bone script, clerical script, large seal script, and small seal script, to the creation of simplified characters since the New Culture Movement. They have gradually shifted to being more phonetic rather than purely pictographic, thus avoiding some of the drawbacks of traditional complex characters, which were more pictographic and less phonetic.

Many modern Chinese words are borrowed from Japanese. The Japanese developed new Chinese words through their understanding of Chinese, combined with modernization reforms. Therefore, much of the Chinese we learn today is essentially a translated version of Japanese, differing significantly from ancient Chinese.

Why is Chinese so difficult to learn? I believe Chinese encompasses various rules such as "sound, shape, meaning, tone, rhythm, context, format, and connotation," among others, with some finer details yet to be fully covered. Here, "sound" refers to phonetics, "shape" to the form of characters, "meaning" to the semantics, "tone" to the intonation, "rhythm" to the cadence, "context" to the situational context, "format" to the structural and stylistic format, and "connotation" to affirmation or negation. The interplay of these numerous rules creates significant challenges in mastering the language. I will delve into these issues one by one in the following sections.

2. Ambiguity in Pinyin Pronunciation

First, let's discuss pronunciation. In Mandarin, pronunciation currently follows a consonant-vowel (initial-final) structure. The pronunciation of a Chinese character involves a blended "transitional sound," where the mouth transitions from the shape for the initial consonant to the shape for the final vowel, with tonal changes applied as well.

This approach inherently leads to ambiguous pronunciation. Unlike English consonants, Chinese initials often have a slight vowel sound at the end. This is evident when you memorize the pinyin chart in elementary school, where the initial consonants are actually pronounced with a vowel sound. When this vowel sound from the initial blends with the actual vowel of the final, it creates a problem of "consecutive vowels." In English, such consecutive vowel sounds are rare because they lead to unclear pronunciation.

Additionally, there are subtle differences like front and back nasal sounds, and flat versus curled tongue sounds, which are hard to distinguish even with careful tongue control. These subtle differences make it difficult for many people to speak standard Mandarin accurately, often leading to misinterpretation.

Chinese cannot quickly output syllables. Each character has one syllable and cannot be slurred. Slurring would make the speech hard to understand. For a person who speaks standard Mandarin, the fastest speaking speed is about 200 characters per minute. Each Chinese character, due to its tonal nature, takes as long to pronounce as a long vowel in English. This means that each Chinese character's pronunciation time is equivalent to the time needed to pronounce an English long vowel, limiting the speed of speech.

In contrast, the fastest speaking speed in English can reach 800-1200 words per minute. This is because many English syllables are pronounced continuously without significant pauses in between, the syllables are shorter, and there are no prominent tonal restrictions.

3. Too Many Homophones

The phonetic system of Chinese is quite limited in its variety of sounds. There are 23 initial consonants (b, p, m, f, d, t, n, l, g, k, h, j, q, x, zh, ch, sh, r, z, c, s, y, w) and 24 final vowels (a, o, e, i, u, ü, ai, ei, ui, ao, ou, iu, ie, üe, er, an, en, in, un, ün, ang, eng, ing, ong), along with some special combinations like ia, iang, and iao. Additionally, there are four tones: high level, rising, falling-rising, and falling.

Using a simple multiplication method, we can estimate that the total number of possible pinyin syllables is around 2500 (23 initials × 24 finals × 4 tones). However, the number of commonly used Chinese characters is about 6000. This means that, on average, each syllable corresponds to about three different characters. In everyday communication, this requires constant disambiguation of which character a spoken syllable represents, which can be quite burdensome. In contrast, English has more syllable combinations and fewer homophones, making it less likely to misinterpret words based on sound alone.

The limited variety of pinyin combinations also leads to a lack of richness in phonetic expression. Some combinations that could theoretically exist are not used because they would sound unclear or inelegant. For example, the internet slang "giao" is essentially a variation of "gao." The initial "g" in pinyin is not a pure consonant, as it contains an implicit vowel sound at the end. When combined with the vowel "ao," it creates a string of three vowels, which is not in line with linguistic rules where consonant-vowel combinations are clearer.

When looking up a word in a dictionary by its pronunciation, you will find numerous homophones, making the process slow and inefficient. We often have to sift through many entries to find the correct character. Similarly, in conversation, we must rely on context to determine which character a given sound represents. People frequently need to ask for additional context or commonly associated words to clarify which character is being referred to, causing unnecessary complications.

4. Limited Combinatorial Possibilities

Some argue that the world operates on mathematical principles, with mathematical mechanisms underlying various phenomena. The great mathematician Alan Turing once showed a picture resembling a cow's pattern, claiming it was generated by a mathematical formula, which people initially thought was a joke. However, we now know that such patterns can indeed be described and generated mathematically. What appears to be naturally random often follows certain mathematical laws, which most people are unaware of. In fact, the application of mathematics in modern science is almost ubiquitous, whereas philosophy, aside from its literary aspects, is essentially a form of science—albeit an imprecise hybrid. Any scientific discipline needs to be described using mathematical models to ensure accuracy; otherwise, it remains a subjective humanistic conjecture. Mathematics helps us filter out the speculative elements of philosophy, bringing it closer to scientific rigor.

If we consider the human brain as an algorithmic machine, then language is the object of its computation. The brain's biological nature leads to inherent instability, resulting in outputs that do not always conform to precise algorithms—unlike computers. The human brain is subject to various biological constraints, making it impossible to execute algorithms with complete accuracy, such as calculating square roots. This inherent imprecision often puts us in difficult situations.

From a mathematical perspective, a character or word can be understood as a combination of symbols. Different combinations convey different meanings, and there should ideally be a one-to-one correspondence between written symbols and their abstract concepts. Concepts can be described through language, but language itself is not the concept—it merely represents it. This can be demonstrated through translation among different languages: although the words differ, the underlying abstract concepts are generally similar, with variations in descriptive precision and emphasis.

English words, in this context, can be seen as a mapping between sets of numbers and abstract concepts. Consider the hexadecimal system: when Arabic numerals are insufficient, we use letters to represent numbers. If we hypothetically did away with Arabic numerals, English words could be seen as enumerations in a 26-base system. This mathematical regularity makes English a simple and easy-to-learn language. From an algorithmic or intelligence perspective, English aligns well with the brain's recognition mechanism, or rather, the brain adapts well to the inherent mathematical structure of English.

In contrast, Chinese, with its abundance of homophones and indistinguishable words, poses significant challenges. The need to continuously disambiguate meanings leads to increased "irrationality" in our thinking processes, with errors perpetually lurking in our minds unnoticed, creating an illusion of inherent confusion.

For example, consider using 26 letters to form words. Ignoring pronunciation, three letters can create 17,576 (26^3) different combinations. Each additional letter exponentially increases the number of combinations without significantly increasing complexity. In Chinese, however, forming a three-character word is much more complex, and handwriting is considerably slower. Each Chinese character's pronunciation, if written in pinyin, would require three to four letters on average, making a three-character combination roughly equivalent to using a dozen letters.

Comparing this mathematically: for the same length of syllables, three Chinese characters in pinyin might span about ten letters. So, the number of combinations of 2500 phonetic syllables cubed (2500^3) versus the number of combinations of 26 letters to the tenth power (26^10) shows a clear difference in combinatorial richness. Although precise quantification is challenging due to the fundamental differences, it's evident that English offers more combinations within a limited length.

Moreover, creating new conceptual words by arbitrarily combining Chinese characters often results in meanings unrelated to the new word, causing the issue of "misalignment between form and meaning." The excess of homophones leads to "misalignment between sound and meaning," destabilizing the phonetic, visual, and semantic coherence of Chinese. This necessitates relying on tones, rhythms, context, fixed poetic formats, and so on for clarification, making it difficult to accurately infer meanings from spoken words alone. A common saying goes, "Understand the words by their sound, just like understanding a drum by its beat," indicating the need to interpret meaning through expression and gestures, complicating communication unless everyone becomes a natural performer, which is unrealistic.

Culturally, Chinese people tend to disdain performers, considering them artificial, pretentious, or even mentally unstable. This aversion likely stems from the misalignment between the tonal system of the language and emotional expression. Exaggerated gestures while speaking can appear as poor theater, evident in many folk performance troupes. Thus, Chinese people prefer ambiguous expression over awkward behavior, avoiding appearing theatrical, which lowers performers' social standing.

This internal contradiction is hard to resolve, except in written communication, which is time-consuming and laborious. People's interactions are based on vague language and constrained body language, making mutual understanding and cooperation nearly impossible. Consequently, in sports that require teamwork, Chinese athletes often underperform, excelling primarily in individual or small-team events like table tennis, women's volleyball, diving, and gymnastics.

5. Discrepancy Between Tones and Emotions

Mandarin Chinese imposes tonal requirements on pronunciation, which can be seen as a problematic aspect of the language. Human expression is inherently emotional, and emotions are closely tied to intonation. Studies have shown that changes in intonation during speech can limit rational thinking and stimulate emotional responses. When comparing with English, for example, words like "damn" or "bitch" that express discontent are pronounced with a falling tone, clearly conveying the speaker's anger, as such emotions are often associated with downward movements like smashing or hitting. Conversely, rising intonations used for questions typically correlate with upward movements like raising one's head, eyebrows, or looking upwards.

In Mandarin, due to the limited variety of pinyin combinations and the prevalence of homophones, tones were added to differentiate meanings. However, this addition is still insufficient, revealing one of the core issues with this phonetic system. Often, the tone required for a word does not match the intended emotional expression. For example, the phrase "去你妈的" (literally "go to your mother," an expression of anger akin to "fuck you") ends with a prolonged first tone on "妈," giving it a declarative feel rather than an angry one. In contrast, "去你大爷的" (a similarly offensive phrase) ends with "大爷" in the fourth tone, a falling tone, conveying decisiveness and matching the intended emotion more accurately.

The critical point here is that the human brain functions as an algorithmic interpreter. It's not that artificial intelligence simulates human thought; rather, the human brain has evolved through a series of algorithms to develop intelligence. The brain itself runs these algorithms, although we have yet to fully understand many of these mechanisms. Language, as the medium of thought, is processed by the brain, and the ambiguous nature of Mandarin as an "input" makes accurate analysis difficult, leading to numerous problems and frequent errors in thought and communication.

6. Difficulties with Radical Lookup

When learning Chinese, students often rely on radicals and character shapes to look up words in dictionaries. This process involves counting the remaining strokes after identifying the radical, which is slow and prone to mistakes. Sometimes the radical isn't obvious; it could be on the left (or top) side, or on the right (or bottom) side, and occasionally the first stroke serves as the radical. If characters with the same radical were grouped together, it could result in too many characters in one category, making it necessary to flip through pages to find the correct one. This counterintuitively slows down the lookup process. As a result, the need to reduce repetitive lookups has introduced uncertainty in identifying radicals, leaving students often confused about which part of the character is the radical.

In contrast, English words and phrases resemble a base-26 numerical system. Words in an English dictionary are ordered alphabetically, allowing for quick and easy lookup by comparing the position of letters in the sequence. For example, "absolute" will always come before "abuse." By comparing the sequence of letters until the first difference, one can quickly determine whether to flip forward or backward in the dictionary. There's no need for extensive categorization, and all words are arranged in a single, unchanging sequence.

While modern electronic dictionaries with handwriting and Wubi input methods can alleviate the slow lookup problem of paper dictionaries to some extent, students without access to electronic dictionaries will still find it laborious. The potential negative impacts of using electronic devices for learning are also worth considering.

7. Inconvenience in Writing

Chinese characters have many strokes, which generally move in horizontal, vertical, left-slanted, and right-slanted directions. Although the writing process seems to follow a top-to-bottom, left-to-right pattern and adheres to strict stroke order rules, it lacks consistency. The conflicting directions of the strokes—up, down, left, right—increase the movement distance and time, as well as the difficulty of writing.

The structure of Chinese characters is difficult to grasp accurately. Some characters have many strokes, while others have few. Traditionally, characters with more strokes were written larger, and those with fewer strokes were written smaller. However, standardized writing grids and computer screens now require all characters to be the same size. This creates a problem where characters with many strokes, like "繁" (complex), "霸" (hegemon), and "霰" (sleet), appear crowded, while characters with fewer strokes, like "广" (broad) and "飞" (fly), leave empty spaces.

Visually, many strokes in Chinese characters are connected but must be written separately, requiring the writer to lift and place the pen frequently, which slows down the writing speed. Consequently, styles like semi-cursive (行书) and cursive (草书) script were invented to simplify writing by merging strokes. However, this introduces another issue—difficulty in recognition. Many calligraphic works are nearly unrecognizable without specialized study or familiarity. This connected style of writing attempts to emulate the Western cursive method but cannot entirely break free from the internal structure of the characters. Therefore, calligraphy becomes another repetitive learning burden, where mastering standard script (楷书) basics is followed by learning various distortions to transition into semi-cursive or cursive, sacrificing some accuracy. This does not significantly improve efficiency and even leads to campaigns promoting "speak standard Mandarin, write standardized characters" to combat illegible handwriting.

Writing Chinese characters inherently contains an element of "violence." For instance, in the Hong Kong movie "The Storm Riders," there is a scene where the Sword Saint, in his younger days without profound skill, writes an ordinary semi-cursive challenge letter. But by the final battle, his challenge letter is in flamboyant cursive. This movie captures the essence of Chinese character writing. The act of writing Chinese characters is akin to a "slashing" action, reflecting the destructive and primal side of the Chinese psyche, hinting at a form of violence and savagery. This stands in stark contrast to the smooth and refined writing systems of Western languages, symbolizing "violent culture" versus "rational culture."

8. Dialect Barriers

Dialects are essentially the products of different groups of people in specific environments forming unique "language markets." As people communicate, their language evolves and adapts, leading to various versions of Chinese. In essence, dialects are the consensus reached among local smart individuals, providing an advantage in communication for those using specific pronunciations and intonations, making exchanges more convenient. Many dialect words are akin to slang in English, functioning as a type of "code" understood only by locals. The author believes that the emergence of dialects is a collective response to the inherent shortcomings of Mandarin, utilizing regional wisdom to create unique vocabularies and grammatical patterns.

People often find their feet unattractive because they compare them to hands, which are more flexible and aesthetically pleasing. Feet are seen as "degraded" versions of hands, a notion evident in our close relatives, chimpanzees, whose feet are quite hand-like with developed thumbs for grasping. Dialects are similarly seen as degraded forms of Mandarin. Many expressions in Mandarin do not apply to dialects, and dialects lack the richness of Mandarin. Due to their regional limitations, dialects cannot compete with Mandarin, much like how feet are secondary to hands. Dialects are thus primarily used at the "grassroots" level.

Why, then, do people in certain regions resist speaking the more "advanced" Mandarin? This resistance stems from the environmental dependency of this perceived superiority. Grassroots Chinese people deal with affairs and face cultural environments far less sophisticated than those associated with "hands." For example, high-level cultural activities like concerts, art exhibitions, and stage plays are rare, while Mandarin is prevalent only in television programs. Therefore, speaking Mandarin feels like mimicking television, equating Mandarin with "acting." Given that many Chinese dramas are highly fictional, using this "acting" language in real life is akin to lying, leading to discomfort or even anger. Consequently, Chinese basic education sees a strange phenomenon where children speak Mandarin in class and switch to dialects outside, becoming accustomed to alternating between "falsehood" and "reality."

In some regions, dialect pronunciation and grammar are nearly foreign languages, such as Cantonese, Shanghainese, Hakka, and Minnan. These dialects are unintelligible to outsiders, creating a form of resistance against top-down governance. Locals often resist the official promotion of Mandarin, embodying the proverb "a strong dragon cannot suppress a local snake."

In temporary or localized cultural systems that can partially avoid the pitfalls of Chinese, social ecosystems can still function normally. For instance, the dialect systems in Fujian and Guangdong, the Shaanxi-Gansu-Ningxia language system in the northwest, the Sichuan-Chongqing language system, and northeastern dialects have gradually formed stable local linguistic ecosystems, with fewer errors in economic activities. However, cities with diverse populations often experience more misunderstandings, leading to amusing incidents.

For example, there was a televised report about a civil servant who was transferred to work in a different region. In his original vocabulary, the word "搞" (gǎo) meant "to handle" or "to do" something. However, in the new location, "搞" had acquired a special connotation, implying romantic entanglement. When this official, who frequently used "搞," interacted with locals, it often led to misunderstandings and dissatisfaction. These grassroots people, not equipped to understand these linguistic differences from a higher perspective, developed inexplicable resistance. Realizing the issue, the official had to consciously avoid using such terms, inadvertently complicating communication. The saying "one's hair has turned grey by the time they return home" illustrates the difficulty of changing a language system ingrained since childhood.

9. The Challenge of Creating New Characters

It is widely known that English is considered the most universal and straightforward language, while Chinese is one of the most difficult languages to learn. So, where does the problem lie? The origins of Chinese characters date back thousands of years, potentially as early as the Shang Dynasty's oracle bone script, believed to have been developed to record the patterns on turtle shells cracked during divination. Over a long history, people continuously invented and accumulated thousands of Chinese characters.

The creation of Chinese characters essentially boils down to four basic strokes: horizontal, vertical, left-falling, and right-falling, similar to the patterns on a turtle shell. This system harbors a fundamental issue: a character can only accommodate a limited number of strokes. Clearly, too many strokes make writing cumbersome and memorization more difficult. As more characters are created, the task of inventing new ones becomes increasingly challenging, hindering the creation and dissemination of new concepts.

Theoretical innovation inevitably involves linguistic innovation. Language is a mapping system where words composed of different syllables correspond to abstract meanings. The phonetic-graphic-meaning system of Chinese results in unstable word meanings, with rules that cannot be fully extended in any direction. Often, meanings are determined by usage habits, with many expressions not following strict logic.

New things emerge constantly, making it difficult to name them. In English, a few letters can be combined to create a new word easily. However, creating a new Chinese word involves combining existing characters, which often do not correspond to new concepts. This requires adding new meanings to old characters, complicating the understanding of word meanings and potentially rendering old words obsolete. If one considers creating a new character, it must account for the "three components": sound, form, and meaning. Given the limited square space for stroke combinations, most simple characters have already been invented, while complex ones are hard to fit. The limited number of distinguishable sounds means homophones are almost unavoidable. Thus, the meaning of a new character is often unclear from its "sound, form, and meaning," significantly increasing the learning difficulty.

In contrast, English's root and associative word-formation system is well-known. These roots abstractly and uniquely define concepts. The cost of creating new words in English is very low; adding a few letters can form a new word. By following pronunciation rules and avoiding repetition, new words can be created by extending syllables. While some argue that Chinese words can also be extended to create new terms, it is evidently more challenging to extend a Chinese word than an English one. Extending a syllable only adds pronunciation, whereas extending a Chinese word incorporates unnecessary elements, complicating the process further.

10. The Headache of Naming

Due to the constraints of Chinese character rules, finding a name that is meaningful, unique, phonetically pleasing, short, and clear has become a very complex task. English does not have such difficulties. A new word can easily be created by rearranging a few syllables and letters. However, Chinese characters cannot be arbitrarily combined like letters. Individual letters do not carry meaning, and each Chinese character is essentially a word. Combining words to create new ones can lead to a structurally chaotic and contradictory outcome. Thus, naming in Chinese is a significant challenge. Without creating new characters, the only option is to add new meanings to existing characters, which can cause confusion and potentially severe consequences.

Can we create a new character? If a new character is invented, not only does the Xinhua Dictionary need to be updated, but also all electronic devices' character libraries would need modification. This would render many old character sets incompatible, unable to display the new character correctly, leading to an even higher cost.

A clear example of this issue is the naming of Chinese aircraft carriers. The Beiyang Fleet had already used up many good names, such as "Zhenyuan" and "Dingyuan." Nowadays, we resort to naming aircraft carriers after provinces, which lacks the expected grandeur. Additionally, since the navy crew members aboard come from all over the country, they work for the nation, yet the fortress they work on bears the name of a specific province, which might not be their hometown. This could create an emotional disconnect between the crew and their aircraft carrier, possibly leading to a gradual "alienation" in their mindset.

Another example is the naming of small flying devices like quadcopters. The term "无人机" (drone) is already used for military drones. Calling them "低慢小飞行器" (low, slow, small aircraft) feels too lengthy. The term "四轴飞行器" (quadcopter) isn't foolproof either. If similar devices with three or two axes appear, this would create legal loopholes. Using random characters for names might seem like nonsensical gibberish.

Consider terms like "quark" and "quantum" in physics. These were translated after being established abroad. If Chinese scholars had first coined "quark," it might have been named "微元" (micro-element), indicating a fundamental particle within an atom. "Quark" sounds arbitrary in Chinese; "夸" (praise) and "克" (conquer) are verbs unrelated to fundamental particles. Hence, many translated foreign names feel genius in their character combinations, something Chinese might never naturally produce.

In conclusion, naming new concepts in Chinese involves adding new meanings to existing characters, which complicates understanding and necessitates extensive annotation. This is contrary to efficient knowledge dissemination. In such a language system, the spread of new concepts disrupts old ones, leading to chaos. To avoid this, a unified authoritative language system is needed, embodying the seeds of violence and despotism. Hence, Chinese people's freedom often remains an internal idea, constrained by cultural and linguistic limitations, resulting in a constant clash between chaotic thinking and harsh natural laws. Any minor mistake can have amplified and terrifying consequences.

11. The Confusion of Abbreviations

In some places, institutions or locations with multiple hierarchical levels often use abbreviations. These abbreviations usually take the first character from each part of the term, which, to those unfamiliar with the full term, can seem like jargon or a code. For instance, "中消协" might be recognized by those familiar with it as "中国消费者协会" (China Consumers Association), while others might mistake it for "中国消防协会" (China Fire Protection Association), depending on how well the term is known. Given the nature of Chinese, a character's meaning often depends on context. Abbreviations remove this context, making the meaning unclear. Thus, familiar usage is relied upon to determine the meaning. If someone does not take care to explain the full original term during dissemination, it is easy for misunderstandings to arise.

In contrast, English abbreviations typically take the initial letters of each word in a long phrase. These combinations strive to avoid duplicating previous abbreviations. If you do not recognize an English abbreviation, you would need to look up the original phrase online, rather than guess its meaning. This ensures the accuracy of knowledge dissemination.

12. The Vicious Cycle of Euphemisms

Chinese places a strong emphasis on euphemisms, a product of the hierarchical values of the feudal era. People were expected to avoid directly naming individuals who were older or held higher status, using other terms instead to show respect. Similarly, negative terms were often replaced with more pleasant-sounding ones. For example, "厕所" (toilet) became "洗手间" (washroom) or "卫生间" (restroom), and "手纸" (toilet paper) was replaced with "卫生纸" (sanitary paper). However, in the human mind, no matter what new term is used as a euphemism, it ultimately gets attached to the original meaning. The negative connotations of the original term will eventually be associated with the new euphemism. Over time, when a new euphemism is widely used, it will be replaced with another term, and after a long period, people might revert to the original term, thus going full circle without finding a suitable, stable name.

The names used for euphemisms originally have their own meanings. Changing their use arbitrarily can confuse those unfamiliar with the terms, making it hard to discern the true meaning. For instance, "如厕" (go to the toilet) has been euphemistically called "方便" (convenient), which originally meant "conditions are suitable." This leads to widespread misunderstandings and jokes, such as the famous one about a foreigner learning Chinese: "我方便的时候不会客" (I won't receive guests when I'm convenient).

13. Homophones in Chinese Characters

When studying classical Chinese literature in middle school, textbooks often highlight numerous "homophones," leaving students puzzled. Given that the texts cited in these books are typically "classics" penned by renowned authors, why didn't they use the characters that perfectly fit the intended meaning? As previously mentioned, the creation of Chinese characters is a challenging process. The characters we use today are the result of long-term development and accumulation. Before the formation of classical or modern Chinese, authors might not have had corresponding characters at their disposal. Alternatively, the "homophones" in classical texts might simply represent phonetic sounds, with the actual meaning derived from the context. In such cases, the phonetic aspect of the character takes precedence over its form.

This apparent "imprecision" was tolerated in the writings of ancient Chinese authors. Addressing this issue would require the creation of new characters—a task far more arduous and complex than interpreting homophones through context. As previously mentioned, creating new characters is difficult, and it's more practical to explain the meaning of a homophone through its context than to invent a new character. Hence, ancient Chinese scholars often settled for using homophones, as they were limited by the cultural framework of their time and had limited capacity for innovative design outside the existing system of characters.

14. Imagery Overload and Lack of Logic

The Chinese language often emphasizes documentation and commentary, as seen in classical Chinese literature such as the "Twenty-Four Histories," the "Four Books and Five Classics," "Records of the Grand Historian," and the "Spring and Autumn Annals." This blend of literature and history is termed "wen shi bu fen jia" (literature and history are inseparable). Similarly, Chinese poetry and prose often consist of a series of related images lacking logical coherence.

Over the long course of cultural development, certain words and phrases have been endowed with positive connotations, and landmarks have been given refined meanings by scholars and poets. Essentially, these are the result of the brain's associative recall from extensive reading—a cultural atmosphere lacking logical connections. In other words, Chinese culture emphasizes "associative logic" rather than "formal logic." When these associations are woven into writing, they often conform to specific literary formats (such as adhering to the requirements of seven-character or five-character quatrains, specific poetic forms, rhyme schemes, etc.), creating a uniformity in style. This makes the literature appealing and rhythmically pleasant at first glance, but upon deeper examination, there is often little substantive content. The writing tends to be filled with subjective and vague personal feelings, lacking definitive meaning.

For contemporary writers, creating similar literary works has become increasingly difficult. The number of aesthetically pleasing and meaningful word combinations is limited, and most of these have already been explored by previous authors. As a result, the potential for developing better verses diminishes, often forcing writers to resort to quoting or plagiarizing earlier works.

15. The Complex and Awkward System of Context

How many languages does a Chinese person need to learn? The answer is at least four. Why is this the case? Due to the inherent ambiguities of Chinese characters, people have gradually developed different phonetic vocabularies and dialects, which vary significantly across regions. Dialects can differ markedly within just a few hundred kilometers. The current standard Mandarin is based on the dialects of the northeastern and Hebei regions, while people in other areas still speak their local dialects. In some regions, the dialects are so distinct that learning Mandarin doesn't necessarily mean one can understand them. Although they share the same written Chinese characters, oral communication is not possible without a period of learning. Many dialects have vocabulary and grammatical rules absent in Mandarin, or their expressions do not conform to the rules of Mandarin.

Since the "New Culture Movement," Chinese intellectuals have gradually developed a new cultural system without abandoning Chinese characters, leading to the evolution of modern Chinese literature. Many new words were invented or borrowed, with many terms translated from Japanese. Essentially, modern Chinese has diverged significantly from classical Chinese. During the Republic of China era, the political center was in the south, and there was no unified official language, although southern accents predominated. Since the founding of the People's Republic of China, Mandarin, primarily based on the northeastern and Hebei dialects, has been enforced nationwide.

To accelerate integration with the international community, China has introduced English education in compulsory schooling since the reform and opening-up period. Many students start learning English from the third grade, with some even beginning in the first grade. As a result, a Chinese person from birth to university graduation is exposed to their local dialect, classical Chinese, modern Chinese, and English. These systems overlap and intersect with different rules and applications, creating a heavy burden even before stepping out of the country.

Language is a tool for thinking, and cultivating clear thinking in such a chaotic linguistic environment seems almost impossible unless one is a genius. Mandarin is considered one of the hardest languages to speak accurately, with difficult distinctions between front and back nasal sounds, inconsistencies between tones and emotional expressions, varying syllable lengths, and numerous homophones. Dialects can compensate for Mandarin's difficulties in pronunciation and clarity. However, some Mandarin words cannot be "localized" well into dialects, resulting in a mix of dialect and Mandarin words that feels as awkward as inserting Chinese words into an English sentence.

16. Spoken and Written Language

Why do Chinese people distinguish between spoken and written language? According to a foreign experiment, an advanced Chinese speaker can read aloud about 200 Chinese characters per minute, while the world record for English is around 1,200 words per minute. This Guinness World Record might even be broken again. Regardless of the semantic density of English and Chinese words, such slow verbal output in everyday communication is quite frustrating. Sometimes, by the time someone finishes speaking, the listener has already guessed the point. To make communication more convenient, spoken language has simplified many of the written rules and removed many idioms, making expression more colloquial and allowing people with different levels of education to communicate basically. For example, during Chinese New Year, you often hear phrases like "值此新春佳节来临之际" ("On the occasion of the New Year"). The origin of such phrases is unknown, but they have become set expressions because people find them appropriate. However, no one would use such phrases in casual conversation; greeting someone with "大爷过年好" ("Happy New Year, sir") is more natural and endearing. Different expressions are used for different contexts, and although they have the same meaning, they are not interchangeable.

Moreover, many written words are rarely used, but their pronunciation might be common. This brings us back to the issue of limited phonetic combinations. The brain determines the meaning through pronunciation, but the meanings of written words and their pronunciations can differ significantly. Understanding written vocabulary can be mentally taxing, especially for illiterate individuals who might never have heard some words. Instead, they might recognize other words with the same pronunciation, leading to misunderstandings. Thus, using written language in spoken communication only works among highly educated individuals. When used with lower social classes, it becomes meaningless.

If an unfamiliar English word is used in conversation, the listener will remember its pronunciation and try to figure out its spelling, then find out its meaning. They won't confuse it with other known words that sound the same, because homophones are rare in English.

The formal written language system in Mandarin is almost unusable in daily life. Speaking Mandarin signifies a different communication system, changing the context and seeming pretentious, excluding ordinary people's everyday emotions. Mandarin is a political language, a tool of governance, with an implicit logic reflecting the power relationship between the upper and lower levels. Those who master Mandarin hold the discourse power. Dialects represent local interest groups that inherently resist the upper levels. The phrase "The mountains are high, and the emperor is far away" reflects how ordinary people don't feel compelled to listen to distant authority. This breeds a subconscious resistance to the culture carried by Mandarin, preventing the dissemination of excellent cultural knowledge at the local level. People continue to uphold local characteristics, leading to policies being implemented superficially while fundamentally protecting local interests. Local authorities are always busy dealing with the directives from above, while the upper levels struggle to understand the local situation, creating a frustrating structure.

17. Why People Don't Like Using Idioms

Due to the inherent instability in the habitual use of the Chinese language, many descriptions require extensive contextual references for clarification. When these contexts form relatively fixed structures and are repeatedly used, they extract key four-character phrases to create new words. These words represent entire stories and do not always conform to grammatical rules, known as "chengyu" (idioms). The term "chengyu" itself means words that have become fixed due to habitual use. However, the "story-like" nature of idioms means that when people use an idiom, the situation they want to express may not align with the original story. Since events rarely repeat in exactly the same way, using idioms can lead people to focus on the idiom's original context rather than the intended meaning. This creates a contradiction: on one hand, idioms simplify expression; on the other hand, they may not convey the precise meaning intended. This makes using idioms challenging and even makes speaking difficult.

Additionally, there is an absurd outcome where people's thoughts tend to gravitate towards familiar things because familiarity provides a sense of security. This idiom culture makes everyone lean towards the situations described by the idioms, forming a cultural constraint. If you want to innovate, people often feel that new things cannot be accurately described, leading to misunderstandings. Thus, it is better to follow past methods, reducing many obstacles in terms of both experience and expression. Gradually, a pattern forms where traditional methods proceed smoothly, while new and unique approaches fail to gain

traction.

18. Post-Hoc Understanding

The Chinese language's propensity for ambiguity is omnipresent in daily life. A major reason for this is the language's tendency to generate "post-hoc understanding" ambiguities. In the process of thinking, people essentially create a context, but without sufficient time to refine the meaning of their sentences. Often, after speaking, they realize that some necessary qualifiers are missing, causing the context to shift from their original intent, leading to different interpretations by others.

When Chinese people discuss a problem, due to this "post-hoc understanding" ambiguity, you will notice that they struggle to stay focused on a serious topic for an in-depth discussion. During the conversation, irrelevant meanings constantly emerge, causing the discussants to deviate from their original thoughts and shift to other topics. Sometimes, certain remarks may imply disrespect, causing discomfort and even leading to grudges, reducing future discussion opportunities.

In such a challenging communication environment, achieving quick, precise, and effective communication is nearly impossible, and errors can occur at any moment. We know that one primary mode of social activity involves many people sparking ideas through smooth communication, continually advancing their collective endeavors. This is very difficult to achieve in China. The best choice for everyone is to operate within an already stable mode, as familiarity with old practices reduces the need for extensive communication. Simply following the established rules and procedures suffices. This collective "unconscious" behavioral pattern is very common in China. People prefer to continually repeat past traditions, and once a process is established, it is hard to change due to the enormous "explanation costs." Unless there is a large-scale unified action from the top, any minor change will face numerous obstacles. This may be one of the reasons why it is so difficult for us to make progress.

19. Fuzzy Understanding

In recent years, the development of artificial intelligence has been rapid, with AlphaGo's victory over human Go masters shocking the world. From the perspective of AI scientists, it is actually surprising that humans can win at all. If we say that artificial intelligence is simulating the human brain, then when AI surpasses the human brain, who is really simulating whom? If we compare the human brain to an intelligent computer, its performance is already far inferior to that of AI. Can we abstract the concept of "intelligence" such that, whether it is artificial or the natural human brain, both are simulating an ultimate intelligence, which is a combination of algorithms, foresight, and analytical capabilities?

From a language analysis perspective, it is evident that the arrangement and combination of English letters are more suited to computer algorithms, as permutations and combinations are inherently mathematical models. Chinese, however, is not like this. The creation of Chinese characters already shows significant difficulties, and relying on permutations and combinations of characters can lead to issues of mixed meanings, contradictions, and miscommunications. Many old words have already had their meanings "occupied," leading to clear problems of semantic overlap and confusion, which are difficult to resolve. Both artificial and human analysis of semantics are challenging to grasp, making daily communication difficult. Chinese language users are always subject to numerous inconsistent rules related to sound, form, meaning, tone, rhythm, context, style, connotations, and more, unlike English, which has fixed, mathematical-like rules. This creates barriers in music and emotional communication, as simple concepts are hard to define and describe accurately due to excessive irrelevant information, causing cognitive difficulties.

Often, what we say—a sentence or a word—has a fuzzy relationship between its form and sound and is mainly judged by context. Chinese language communication is a storm of ambiguity. Sometimes, we rely on past experiences and the closeness of relationships to determine whether a statement is a joke or a genuine insult.

II. Cultural Ecology

Language is the primary tool for cultural exchange. In this chapter, we will discuss in detail the impact of a flawed linguistic environment on Chinese social and cultural contexts and the current state of affairs that has resulted from it.

1. Cultural Creation and Confusion

The indistinct nature of Chinese words and the difficulty of creating new characters pose obstacles to cultural innovation, limiting people's thinking. Chinese characters are a form of "habitual language," where the rules for expressing meaning are uncertain. This results in meanings that do not reside in pronunciation or form but are instead inferred from context.

Some literary figures might enjoy creating ambiguity, deliberately crafting situations where confusion arises to showcase their literary prowess. Adding new meanings to old words has become a form of cultural innovation. However, this is a detrimental practice that only breeds more confusion.

Latin-based alphabetic languages rarely encounter this problem. Letters themselves have no fixed meaning and only convey sounds. Different combinations of syllables form different words, allowing the creation of new words to express new concepts without repeating past terms. This avoids the chaos of multiple meanings that rely on context for interpretation. While word roots may not have a definite meaning, their pronunciation can trigger associations in the brain, relating to similar-sounding concepts through probabilistic inference based on experience.

English has a far richer variety of phonetic combinations than Chinese. The phonetic system of Chinese characters does not allow for many combinations of syllables, making it challenging to innovate words without lengthening them. However, lengthening a word involves adding characters that may not be related to the concept, and ensuring the pronunciation is relevant is a difficult problem to reconcile. This could lead to a new word comprising characters with meanings almost unrelated to the intended concept. Such difficulties and confusion are the consequences of the Chinese language.

The only solution is to rely on written communication rather than ambiguous spoken language. The endless documentation within Chinese government institutions is a testament to this. Clearly conveying policies without misunderstanding during multiple transmissions is an incredibly challenging task. Chinese people spend their entire lives trying to articulate clearly. When even the basic function of communication is flawed, how can higher-level innovation and creation be achieved? Such endeavors require the accurate and clear exchange of ideas among many people.

2. Loss of Concepts

Language is a tool for thought, and technology is the result of that thought. If there are problems with the thinking tool, it will affect the quality of the outcomes. A major issue with Chinese in the field of technology is the "loss of concepts."

The first problem is translation. Since many technological advancements in modern times were invented by foreigners, their names are primarily in foreign languages, especially from Latin-based languages. This presents a problem in translation: if transliteration is used, it might be better to just use the original foreign word, which isn't true translation. If a semantic translation is used, new concepts often don't have corresponding meanings in Chinese characters. This leads to the creation of new words by combining characters, but these new words often add new meanings to old ones, essentially distorting and altering the original meaning. Such translation actually damages and mutates the culture itself, making it unrecognizable. Moreover, even if translation is possible, it often loses the root meaning and associative significance of the original foreign word, making the translated scientific terms far removed from their original meanings. Science demands precision and accuracy, and under these circumstances, can scientists truly understand the problems?

A striking example is the word "antibody." From its root, it means "against the body," referring to its function of eliminating harmful cells in the body.

However, when translated into Chinese as "抗体" (kàng tǐ), the term "体" might be interpreted as referring to the substance itself as a "body," diverging significantly from the original meaning of "against the body." Can even a very smart person accurately grasp the knowledge through such terms? Exploring the unknown is already fraught with uncertainties, and such translation is like the blind men feeling an elephant.

How can a culturally chaotic and illogical system develop precise, error-free high technology? There is a saying that if an infinite number of monkeys randomly typed on typewriters, given enough time, one would eventually type out all of Shakespeare's works. Chinese scientific research is somewhat similar; it consumes a vast amount of resources but yields very limited output due to internal factors. China has hardly won any Nobel Prizes in science, and even the few successes are usually in the realm of applied science, not in creating groundbreaking, original theories. Chinese culture is suited for recording and commentary, not for innovation, which only leads to more confusion. As previously discussed, the cost of promoting innovation is almost as high as not innovating at all. Therefore, China will remain in the realm of mature technology promotion and application, with deep theoretical inventions and discoveries being nearly impossible. China will continue to be a follower in technological development, always striving to catch up with developed countries and, to put it bluntly, will long remain a "technology scavenger."

3. Valuing Confusion

Due to the inherent contradictions in Chinese culture, Chinese history is a continuous struggle against its own culture. These cultural flaws, present from the outset, unintentionally oppose human nature and rationality, leading to difficulties in achieving significant progress in various aspects of social life. Many things remain in a half-baked state. Chinese culture is rife with nonsense, filled with misconceptions and often mixes unrelated elements together, preventing the development of any deep, logical consistency. This is encapsulated in the phrase "rarely clear, often confused."

The idea of "rarely clear, often confused" suggests a perpetual state of confusion, where clarity is never achieved. To avoid the pain of this confusion, people might embrace it, causing further mental harm. Consequently, rates of depression and mental illness in China are among the highest in the world. Many aspects considered part of human "civilization" struggle to develop smoothly, whether in music, film, or science.

To use a brutal analogy, imagine a person with a necrotic piece of flesh on their left hand that needs to be removed and replaced with healthy flesh from their right leg to prevent overall functional impairment. After such a surgery, the previously necrotic left hand might improve, but the right leg, now missing a piece of healthy flesh, would take a long time to heal. This isn't fair to the right leg, which was originally healthy but had to be sacrificed, while the decaying left hand benefited. Given this, if healthy parts are inevitably cut, it might seem advantageous for the right leg to also become necrotic, hoping to receive flesh from another body part. This mindset indicates that whether the right leg improves or deteriorates depends on the brain's "surgical" decision. Such a chaotic structure forces even the sharp-witted to embrace confusion.

4. Ethical Fixations

It seems that the only remaining pleasure for many Chinese people lies in the complexities of ethics and relationships—issues such as the dynamics between mothers-in-law and daughters-in-law, extramarital affairs, and the less-discussed instances of incest. Additionally, there's the deeply entrenched feudal bureaucratic culture that has persisted for thousands of years. These interpersonal relationship studies are the few areas that still engage Chinese people and can be developed within the scope of human nature.

In other areas, despite their painstaking efforts, many Chinese people encounter an invisible "ceiling" as they mature or complete their university education. If they cannot overcome this cultural barrier by learning Western languages and ways of thinking, or even studying abroad, they may find that their earlier efforts are in vain. They might end up returning to their mundane, intolerable state of being, where life consists of repetitive, mechanical labor with little joy, barring criminal behavior or moral decay.

Most people's thoughts are confined to finding loopholes and ways to bend the rules without getting caught. However, since China is a society where connections and relationships play a crucial role, it's difficult to commit wrongful acts without being noticed. This necessitates the continuous cultivation of interpersonal relationships and the expansion of one's influence to suppress others, ultimately creating a hierarchical structure based on mutual interests.

The higher one's status, the greater their capacity to oppress others and safely engage in wrongdoing.

Thus, a social structure emerges where the actual distribution of benefits is based on one's position within these interpersonal hierarchies. Studying ethics, in essence, becomes an examination of hierarchy and distribution. Consequently, political and family relationships dominate Chinese film and television themes, with palace intrigues combining both aspects, making them a popular source of entertainment.

5. Han Chinese Lack Music

In his show "Xiao Shuo," Gao Xiaosong once remarked, "Han Chinese have no music." As mentioned earlier, modern Chinese inherently includes tonal elements. This creates a significant challenge when singing, as the musical tones of the notes and the tonal inflections of the lyrics can become thoroughly entangled, making it nearly impossible for listeners to accurately discern the lyrics from the song, often leading to misinterpretation.

Additionally, the pronunciation of Chinese characters is transformational, involving the transition from consonants to vowels, with relatively fixed syllable lengths. This is not well-suited to the varying rhythms of music. As a result, Chinese songs often emphasize lyrical content over melodic richness, which is in stark contrast to the essence of music, where melody is the soul. This peculiarity is evident in the ancient Chinese literary form of "ci" (lyric poetry), which was intended to be set to music. However, while the lyrics have been preserved, the melodies have not, indicating that ancient Chinese placed less value on recording melodies.

This dissonance has made it challenging for Chinese popular music to align with international standards. A clear example is that many Chinese songs are covers of Japanese or Korean melodies. Artists like Korea's Lee Jung Hyun and PSY (known as "Bird Uncle") have gained international acclaim, while Chinese songs rarely feature on global download and sales charts. Although there have been occasional instances of fans boosting chart positions, the music itself hasn't received widespread recognition. This may be primarily because Korean and Japanese languages have been adapted to phonetic short-syllable words, more closely aligning with languages like English, allowing greater creative freedom in music composition. In contrast, Chinese is constrained by numerous complex rules.

Moreover, the tonal elements of Chinese phonetics, shapes, and meanings interfere with musical tones, making clear pronunciation difficult. To sing clearly, one must elongate the tones to allow for distinction, but elongating tones prevents the expression of lively rhythms. This results in Chinese songs generally conveying a melancholic mood. The widespread depression among Chinese people might also be related to being in such a repressive environment for extended periods.

Due to the inherent incompatibility between Chinese and music, many songs we find pleasing often contain meaningless onomatopoeic words like "di," "li," "da," and "la." Another example is Jay Chou, who employs a very ambiguous singing style, making it difficult to discern the lyrics. This approach somewhat reconciles the intrinsic issues between Chinese and music, allowing people to focus more on the musical qualities themselves and less on the "interference" of the inherent musicality of the Chinese language. This might be one of the reasons for his music's popularity.

6. Historical Perspective on "Infidelity"

The advent of monogamy marked the end of the "communal" matriarchal clan society of primitive life, transitioning humanity to a patrilineal family inheritance system, forming more stable "family" relationships. This indicates that monogamy is advantageous and better suited for raising the next generation. However, a person's life is long and lonely, and choosing only one partner excludes other possibilities. The author believes that love is a comprehensive reaction in an individual's brain, combining personal experiences and human cultural history, which results in an assessment of a potential mate's ability to adapt to social environments, ultimately choosing what is perceived as the most advantageous "genetic material" to produce offspring deemed superior by instinct. Love is the key to how individuals influence history — it is crucial in determining the nature of offspring.

Due to the randomness of life encounters and the relatively short "window" period for choosing a mate, one might meet someone who better fits their standards after marriage. The strong will to choose the "better" option conflicts with social morality, seriously impacting family stability. Infidelity that does not result in offspring does not significantly affect history, as it is a short-term social activity compared to the enduring and stable nature of marriage.

7. Social Environment and Cancer

China's cancer incidence rate is among the highest in the world, which is closely related to common habits such as smoking, drinking, and the pressures of life. Social customs force people to adapt to these harmful habits.

Exchanging cigarettes and lighting them for each other is a widespread social gesture of friendliness among men. If someone offers you a cigarette and you refuse, claiming not to smoke, you risk distancing yourself from them, making further interaction awkward. To avoid this social pressure, some people reluctantly take up smoking to gain social advantages, often with the false hope that they will not succumb to illness. Unfortunately, when illness does strike, it is often too late for regrets.

Additionally, the saying "wine reveals the truth" suggests that a person's behavior after drinking reveals their true self. However, it is widely understood that being drunk does not necessarily lead to truthfulness; it is often just an excuse for expressing dissatisfaction. Misconduct while drunk can also be excused as a result of the alcohol. Some people can even fake drunkenness to escape social obligations, relying on their acting skills.

Why can't Chinese people adopt healthier Western social habits? Western social gatherings often involve red wine, but producing enough quality red wine for China's large population is nearly impossible, and low-quality red wine is unsuitable for social occasions. Cocktails are another option, but their high cost makes them impractical. As a result, affordable and widely available baijiu (white liquor) becomes the common choice.

Besides smoking and drinking, the generally oppressive living environment is another cancer trigger. People often face oppression from others, and due to various constraints, they cannot change this situation. The suppressed feelings of resentment remain, causing the oppressed to be in a constant state of readiness for conflict, similar to the tension before capturing prey. Laws restrict violent retaliation but do not limit frequent minor oppressions, leaving the oppressed with little recourse. They must endure or risk severe consequences. This continuous tension reduces their immune system's efficiency, leading to chronic diseases and eventually cancer. Even those who conform and align with oppressors do not necessarily escape health issues, as the constant disruptions to their body's balance can be equally detrimental. Thus, under such a system, most people's health deteriorates, with chronic illnesses accumulating and cancer becoming an inevitable outcome.

8. Marriage Among Only Children

The issue of marriage for only children is extremely challenging to resolve because each child is cherished by their family. Parents often invest nearly all their wealth and resources into their child, leading to a generation of pampered individuals. When it comes to choosing a spouse, this means merging and restructuring two entire families, making the stakes incredibly high. Most people find it difficult to bear the consequences of a failed marriage. It's akin to having just one bullet in a gun when aiming at a target—you need a longer time to aim because once the shot is fired, there's no going back. In this context, marriage becomes a gamble, with the outcome of married life with a relatively short-term partner remaining unknown, judged only by recent behavior.

For only children, marriage affects the welfare of three generations within a family, unlike in the past when children from larger families would marry and establish their own households, with less interference from elders.

Another deeper factor is that, after years of reform and development, the social status of women in China has significantly improved, and they have demonstrated strong competitiveness in various fields. However, the majority of Chinese men have not seen a corresponding improvement in their status. Politics seems to be the one area women do not dominate, and the rigidly hierarchical patriarchal political system in China makes it difficult for most men to improve their political and economic status. Consequently, they struggle to attract the pampered single daughters of other families.

A small privileged class controls the majority of resource allocation rights and uses these rights to seize additional economic resources, naturally leading to the acquisition of additional sexual resources. Reports have surfaced of corrupt officials maintaining multiple mistresses, sometimes numbering in the hundreds, while a large number of single men remain. Such extreme imbalance is rare in any country.

9. Why Is Moutai Liquor So Expensive?

In various regions of China, there are local distilleries with their own brands, and drinking local baijiu is an activity that supports the local economy. The high price of Guizhou's Moutai liquor is due to its widely recognized cultural and historical significance.

Firstly, the name itself plays a significant role. Chinese people are inherently influenced by Taoist culture, with legends such as the "Maoshan Taoist" being well-known. "Tai" (台) is an important symbol in Taoist rituals, imperial abdications, and sacrificial ceremonies, as seen in names like "Qixing Tai" (Seven-Star Platform) and "Shouzen Tai" (Abdication Platform). The famous "Temple of Heaven" (Tiantan), representing feudal culture, is essentially a platform (台). From this perspective, the name "Moutai" has a richer cultural connotation compared to "Wuliangye." Although "Moutai" has little to do with either "Mao" (茅) or "Tai" (台) individually, together they form a name associated with high-quality liquor. Whether it's the rituals of Maoshan Taoists or emperors performing sacrifices on a platform, good liquor is always involved. This subtle association influences people subconsciously.

On the other hand, "Wuliangye" (五粮液) literally means "five-grain liquid," referring to the use of five grains—sorghum, rice, glutinous rice, wheat, and corn—as ingredients in its production. Many liquors could be called "Wuliangye" since they also use these five grains. Additionally, Moutai is claimed to be the national liquor of China, with stories of winning awards at the Panama-Pacific International Exposition, which enhances its reputation and gives it a sense of long-standing quality.

The traditional design of Moutai's packaging further contributes to its prestige. Unlike other liquors in glass bottles, Moutai's packaging conveys a sense of "weight" and dignity, making it appear more impressive in social settings. This aligns well with the cultural values of the Chinese people.

Essentially, the primary component of baijiu produced across China is ethanol, with similar chemical compositions and only slight differences in taste. Yet, this harsh and bitter drink is a staple in social interactions, a topic discussed in more detail in the section on drinking culture.

10. Television and Reality

The official discourse system exists on television, whereas daily life operates under a different, local discourse system, making seamless communication in such a cultural environment exceedingly difficult. Civilized ideological concepts are hard to disseminate and remain confined to very small circles. For Chinese people, observing the lives of foreigners is akin to watching a movie—they seem to be "acting." In reality, that is their genuine life, closely mirroring what is shown on TV, forming a culturally integrated whole. Their media provide true reports and express genuine opinions.

In contrast, Chinese media, especially television, filter all information, presenting only content that aligns with certain political aims and ideologies. Naturally, people become aware of the falsity of television, perceiving it like a fictional drama or movie, unrelated to their own lives. When Chinese people watch foreign TV media, they often feel the same sense of falseness—are they acting? Since TV, as a multimedia form that includes sound and images, is a sophisticated means of cultural transmission, it creates a peculiar sense of artificiality and falseness when showing the true lives of foreigners to Chinese viewers. But no, that is indeed their real life.

Chinese people's real lives, however, rarely appear on television because they are deemed mundane and unremarkable. For Chinese viewers, TV media are places of pretense and hypocrisy. Sketches on Chinese TV would never happen in real life.

This pretense and hypocrisy are seen as foreign elements, representing external intrusion and control, a detestable ruling power, something Chinese people instinctively resist. Consequently, many foreign cultural elements conveyed through these media are also rejected. The lives of Chinese people are difficult to change and improve because change and acceptance of foreign culture represent the unknown and uncertainty, bringing risks and even the fear of failure or death. While they might miss out on the benefits of foreign cultures, they believe they won't be deceived, continuing the survival methods validated by their ancestors for thousands of years. They firmly believe that only this way ensures they won't make mistakes, guaranteeing the perpetual survival of their race. But in this ever-changing world, can sticking to old methods forever truly work?

11. Money! Money! Money!

There's a saying that life is like a play, but the Chinese don't seem to live their lives as if they were acting; they are too focused on "reality." They have a natural aversion to more civilized ways. The official discourse system exists only on television and in some formal occasions, rarely being mentioned in daily life. The spiritual world of the Chinese is so monotonous that any complex, advanced form of expression finds no place. People lack singing and dancing, bands and theater groups, and there is very little higher-level spiritual communication. Everyone is constantly accumulating wealth, and the growth of money becomes the only meaningful thing because it signifies more survival resources. The accumulation of wealth seems endless—more houses, more sex, and more offspring, with the saying "People die for wealth, birds die for food" holding true until the end of one's life.

Societal wealth is not just about money but about the integration and utilization of resources. Especially in the realm of technological innovation, which exponentially amplifies the power to create wealth. The recent massive successes of companies like Amazon, Apple, and Microsoft in the United States prove this point. The excessive pursuit of money itself only contributes to capital's wealth effect but does little for genuine wealth creation. When epoch-making products are invented, many existing values collapse in a short period, leading to significant wealth transfers. New wealth replaces old forces, becoming the leaders of the era.

12. Chinese Movies and the Oscars

In early spring 2020, amid the rampage of the novel coronavirus in China, a Korean film about family life, *Parasite*, won four Oscars, making history as a non-English film. One wonders what the Chinese film industry thinks about this. Compared to South Korea, another Asian country, China—a significant film-producing nation—fails to produce Oscar-winning movies. The only award ever received was Jackie Chan's "Lifetime Achievement Award," which was given to him personally and had nothing to do with Chinese cinema.

According to my theory, this is fundamentally related to culture—particularly language. The spiritual world of the Chinese is chaotic, often reflected in the nonsensical dialogue in movies. If you scrutinize these dialogues, you'll find them annoyingly incomprehensible, incompatible with the rational foreign culture, and unrelated to foreign humor. A culture that doesn't value logic has no common ground with other nations. Therefore, many Chinese art forms, such as skits, dances, and galas, are similar to poetry and prose, with chaotic piling up around a theme, lacking clear and organic connections. This often leaves people confused, making it difficult to gain mainstream recognition. Hollywood professionals have spent many years honing their craft and are discerning. To clear out these "grains of sand" and gain their recognition, we need to spend a long time polishing our works.

13. The "Invasion" of Japanese Manga

Japanese manga has been a spiritual sustenance for the generation of Chinese born in the 1980s, captivating them with its exquisite art style and imaginative, emotionally explosive stories. It must be acknowledged that Japanese manga possesses a remarkable aesthetic quality, especially in the detailed depiction of female figures and the meticulous attention to various details. Compared to films, manga may have lower production costs since it requires only paper and pen, allowing for a greater volume of cultural creation. Manga also offers unique abstract simplification effects, impossible to achieve with live-action filming, and utilizes distinctive exaggeration and humor.

The success of Japanese manga likely stems from its long-term development process, involving numerous experimental works where artists learn from each other, innovate, and accumulate various novel techniques. By incorporating the strengths of many, excellent creative methods emerged, leading to the rise of genius manga artists and their classic works.

Some of the naive and straightforward ideas in Japanese manga may seem almost childish to Chinese readers. For instance, the persistent desire for victory in *Saint Seiya* appears incredulous to us. Given the overwhelming strength of the opponents and the apparent lack of any chance of winning, why continue to fight so desperately? Isn't this a path to self-destruction? However, the core theme of the manga is to create possibilities out of the impossible and to achieve miracles through repeated "self-destructive" efforts. Though it may seem childish, it is filled with positive significance. The imaginative plots and stunning character designs offer an escape from the mundane, making these Japanese mangas highly captivating and successful.

14. Religion and Economics

If human thoughts are responses of the brain to external signals, using internal experiences or "algorithms" to derive results, then everything we do is for the future. The only way we influence the future is by changing our actions in the present moment. All our actions accumulate over time to produce corresponding results, much like the compound interest on a loan, where a small initial advantage gradually expands, eventually creating significant differences.

At present, it seems that death is inevitable for everyone, and everything we own will be lost. Does this mean that all our efforts are futile? We cannot be certain of the future; we act based on the limited information we have. The author believes that compared to compound interest, the concept of discounting seems to be a more interesting "algorithm." Our future is not entirely fixed; we can project the future from our current state and make significant efforts to change our present condition, thus altering the discounting of the future and consequently impacting it.

This idea suggests that even the smallest actions we take now can have profound effects and should be taken seriously. Finance and economics involve anticipating and realizing the future. Whoever better predicts future trends and takes actions to position themselves advantageously will gain future benefits. But does all this effort ultimately discount to "0"? Will we eventually lose everything? This line of thought might lead us to lose the courage to act, as it seems all efforts are ultimately in vain, both for individuals and for humanity as a whole.

The author prefers to believe in Christian teachings and has actively participated in the church, becoming a believer. The author thinks that the only reason for all these efforts is the hope that we will ultimately reach a better place—heaven—rather than end up with nothing.

15. Baijiu, Opium, and Smartphones

The saying "Li Bai can compose a hundred poems after a jug of wine" reflects how the intrinsic anti-logical nature of the Chinese character system can lead to inevitable depressive emotions when one is sober, as it is contrary to rationality and even humanity. However, when drinking alcohol, rational thinking decreases, making the rational oppression less apparent. Thus, alcohol brings a sense of relaxation and happiness through reduced rationality and mental confusion, which allows for a novel recombination of words, resulting in creatively inspired poetry.

Similarly, due to this inherent oppression, a sense of spiritual malaise is almost a universal state, making the search for temporary relief an inevitable choice, as long periods are composed of countless short-term intervals. When the only pleasure in life is the pursuit of short-term "comfort," addiction becomes an unavoidable "rational" choice. In the Qing dynasty, opium smoking was widespread among Chinese people. However, why were foreigners less affected by opium? It might be because foreigners had stronger motivations to resist this temptation, or perhaps, in their utility scale, the pleasure brought by opium was not the most intense.

In modern times, a new type of "spiritual opium" is electronic products, including mobile games, short videos, etc. This temporary pleasure can indeed numb the nerves, alleviating immediate pain, but the long-term negative impacts are significant. It makes people lose their fighting spirit, indulging in fleeting pleasures, and losing the persistence for long-term goals, which are the things that hold greater value.

16. The Future of National Essence

Peking opera represents the essence of traditional Chinese stage art, from facial makeup and costumes to singing styles and lyrics, emphasizing "singing, reciting, acting, and fighting," along with unique skills. It encapsulates many classic stories from Chinese history, serving as a cultural treasure of national memory. However, due to the continuous impact of new cultural elements, this pompous and slow-paced art form can no longer compete with the visually stunning and impactful modern screen arts. Moreover, many of the stories are too ancient to have much contemporary relevance, and the values they convey are outdated. The mix of archaic and modern language in performances often feels discordant, and it is almost impossible to create works that resonate with the current era. Thus, Peking opera can only be preserved as a cultural heritage to some extent.

17. The Futility of Kung Fu

Chinese kung fu, as a traditional combat technique, includes many deadly moves such as eye-gouging, throat-locking, and groin attacks. In modern life, these moves are almost impossible to use without facing legal consequences. In an unsafe social environment, learning some self-defense skills might be useful and could help fend off attackers when necessary. However, rather than risking one's life in a fight, it might be more practical to cooperate and avoid harm, or simply be able to run faster than the assailant. After all, the attacker is usually desperate and prepared to fight to the death, while the victim is unprepared, making the odds of winning low. Spending a significant amount of time practicing kung fu to prevent an injury that might happen once in a decade and still not being guaranteed to win seems impractical. It would be more beneficial to train in long-distance running, allowing for a quick escape, which might be the best way to ensure safety.

From a physical exercise perspective, martial arts movements are complex, and the overall activity level is not much different from regular sports. Instead of spending energy learning combat techniques, it might be more practical to focus on general physical fitness. As the saying goes, "Strength fears youth," meaning that in a life-and-death fight, absolute strength often determines the outcome.

18. What to Do About Chinese Soccer

China's soccer teams consist of provincial clubs that usually play in local leagues. For international tournaments, the best players from these clubs are gathered for "training camps" and then assembled into a national team to represent China in world competitions. Soccer is a sport that heavily relies on teamwork and coordination. The national team, composed of around twenty players from different parts of the country, often has members with vastly different backgrounds, personalities, and ways of thinking. Effective coordination during the split-second decisions in a match, such as whether to shoot or pass, attack or defend, requires long-term familiarity and practice. Only players with similar thoughts and personalities can work together seamlessly.

However, this seems to be a significant challenge for the Chinese national team. During a game, players need to think quickly, and since language is a tool for thought, using an unclear or ambiguous language can hinder performance. Even if the players speak Mandarin, they might think in their local dialects. Trying to achieve clarity and unity in such a situation is difficult, which could be one of the reasons why China, despite having a population of over a billion, struggles to produce a successful soccer team.

Therefore, the key to improving China's soccer performance might not lie solely in technical training but in mental training. If possible, adopting the language environment of a soccer-advanced country for training could be beneficial. Countries like the UK, Japan, Germany, Portugal, and Spain could serve as models. After selecting one, a unified foreign language training environment should be used. Coaches should also be chosen from the same language group. Players should be selected based on their proficiency in this foreign language to ensure that little to no translation is needed during training. All relevant soccer terminology, tactics, and player interactions should be conducted in the foreign language. This way, the players' soccer thinking could be entirely transformed into the new language, potentially leading to fundamental improvements in the national team's performance.

19. Women Aren't Afraid of Death

Just as the shape of the universe is determined by black holes, a person's life is ultimately defined by death. An entity without boundaries cannot be defined, and the same goes for life, which is ultimately judged upon death. Death marks the limit of life, and without it, life itself cannot be defined.

For women, death doesn't seem as frightening. As long as their death is reasonable or fitting in some way, they can accept it. This appears to be a mysterious aspect written into women's genes, possibly due to their two X chromosomes, while men have one X and one Y chromosome, the latter containing fewer genes. I once heard some stories that brought this idea to light. A person asked his elderly grandmother about her thoughts on being cremated after death. She simply chuckled without any display of distress. There was also a couple where the man suggested a lover's suicide due to certain circumstances, and the woman agreed. When the time came, she took the poison, but the man got scared and regretted it. In daily life, women often appear more cheerful, confident, and less troubled. For them, the meaning of life lies in living itself, without delving into deeper questions, leaving such complex issues to men to solve.

Religion seems designed for men, with women generally excluded. The fundamental reason might be that women aren't as concerned with the problem of death. For them, life and its end are natural parts of existence, and they don't worry about their own death or ponder this abstract issue. This could be because their chromosomes and genes are more "complete" than those of men. It's possible that chromosomes and genes determine not just physical but also cognitive structures, ultimately influencing philosophical thinking.

Men, more "afraid of death," fixate on this issue because they refuse to accept the inevitable individual demise. They strive to create something enduring to mitigate this sense of loss, leading to the development of deeper religion, science, and culture. Thus, from the fear of death arises a form of immortality. Women focus on their small slice of life, while men consider the broader span of existence and legacy. Genetically speaking, the Y chromosome is incomplete, and the pairing X chromosome inevitably comes from an ancient female ancestor. From this perspective, women carry more of the "material foundation" of heredity, while men compensate for their genetic shortcomings through the cultural transmission of information.

20. Chinese Men Are Inferior

Chinese men lack charm, both spiritually and physically.

Firstly, because Chinese people have black hair, a color that absorbs light and appears dull, without dyeing, any hairstyle lacks a sense of depth and dimension. Additionally, Chinese men generally do not engage in fitness activities, partly due to a lack of facilities. The concentration of residential buildings means most people don't have access to exercise spaces. This results in Chinese men often being either thin or overweight, rarely having a fit and attractive physique.

Spiritually, Chinese men are often seen as dependent on authority, struggling to exhibit "masculine vigor," which symbolizes status and rank and is almost the privilege of leaders. The subservient "eunuch-like" behavior is prevalent.

In terms of intelligence, although many Chinese men are highly intelligent and well-educated, high IQ often correlates with dominant rationality, which contrasts with the emotional love women expect. An intelligent man may have social advantages but is often deemed unsuitable for romantic relationships, making women find them dull. Paradoxically, the higher the IQ, the worse this situation might be.

Furthermore, statistics show that Chinese men's reproductive organs are smaller compared to their Western counterparts, which may not satisfy women's reproductive desires. Some foreign studies suggest that sexual satisfaction is equivalent to gaining $100,000. If this is true, both Chinese men and women are missing out significantly.

In this context, material wealth has become almost the only standard by which Chinese women judge men. Since it is hard to find various qualities that satisfy women in Chinese men, women settle for material fulfillment. Material enjoyment can at least alleviate some of their disappointments. When money becomes the sole criterion for choosing a partner, men's only way to compete for mates is by accumulating wealth. However, in modern society, money is linked to various resources, especially financial ones. To amass significant wealth, one must mobilize a large amount of corresponding social resources, causing a ripple effect. Everyone chasing after money leads to numerous social problems, including disregarding social ethics and harming others' interests through various forms of overt and covert theft. Law enforcement is time-consuming and laborious, with many criminals escaping justice, while the living space for law-abiding citizens becomes increasingly limited.

21. Awkward Entertainment

Local dialects and regional operas were once the main forms of indigenous Chinese art. However, with the progress of modernization, these have largely disappeared. They have been replaced by popular songs and dances created by combining Western artistic theories with modern Chinese cultural systems. These new forms of entertainment seem to be the domain of professional performers, while grassroots artistic creation has vanished.

Due to the issues mentioned earlier, modern artistic expressions rely on the modern language system. At its core, this represents the dominance of foreign culture, suppressing local culture and resources. Following a so-called highbrow route places one in a somewhat opposing stance to the local populace. The outcome is often short-lived, as no one wants to constantly be in an awkward position.

Pure entertainment has also lost its flavor. Pure enjoyment is taboo; performances on stage must primarily promote mainstream culture to maintain a semblance of unity. This leaves people in a perpetual state of internal conflict, torn between their true feelings and the need to conform to the external cultural narrative.

22. The Prevalence of Diabetes and Mental Illness

It is said that the average size of Chinese men's genitalia is only ten centimeters, which is not among the top ranks worldwide. The author speculates that this might be due to longer genitalia being more prone to infections, as the larger mucosal surface area makes it harder for the immune system to fend off viruses. Additionally, the Chinese diet might lack sufficient nutrition, leading to generally weaker physical constitutions. Over long historical periods, those with larger genitalia may have contracted sexually transmitted diseases (STDs) more frequently due to having more sexual partners. Traditional Chinese medicine lacked effective treatments for STDs, which necessitate antibiotics, only introduced to China in modern times. Consequently, many with larger genitalia might have died prematurely from STDs, often before reproducing. This led to a reverse selection, where those with smaller genitalia had a significantly higher survival rate, gradually resulting in the current situation.

Chinese men are unable to fully satisfy Chinese women, leading to widespread sexual frustration among Chinese women, who cannot achieve true sexual fulfillment. Western psychology and Freud's psychoanalytic theory suggest that unfulfilled sexual desires in women can lead to hysteria. This could mean that women with high sexual needs might have a lower survival rate due to hysteria, while those with lower sexual needs are less prone to hysteria and have a higher survival rate.

The reason why female survival rates might not be as affected by STDs is that women have more complete chromosomes than men; the X chromosome contains many more genes than the Y chromosome, potentially offering better resistance to diseases and allowing them to survive longer even with illnesses. These hypotheses lack substantial data support and are based on long-term observations of life phenomena, serving merely as a theoretical analysis.

Following this logic, we end up with a rather depressing outcome: a society full of sexually indifferent women and semi-impotent men. Since sexual satisfaction is unattainable, people turn to food for gratification, potentially explaining the highly developed culinary culture in China. However, overeating can lead to numerous health problems, including diabetes, while sexual repression can cause mental health issues, both prevalent in China. According to data from a well-known online news outlet, as of the end of 2017, there were 243.264 million people with mental disorders in China, a prevalence rate of 17.5%; over 16 million had severe mental disorders, with an incidence rate exceeding 1%, and these numbers are growing annually.

The author obtained data on diabetes prevalence in various Chinese provinces through the internet but could not find specific numbers of mental illness cases, only the number of psychiatric hospital beds, which can be used to estimate the prevalence of mental illnesses to some extent.

Region	Population (thousands)	Diabetes Prevalence (%)	Prediabetes Prevalence (%)	Psychiatric Beds (thousands)	Beds/Population (%)

Inner Mongolia	2539.60	19.90	39.80	1730.00	68.12
Hainan	944.72	17.50	35.00	N/A	N/A
Fujian	3973.00	17.30	49.80	3764.00	94.74
Chongqing	3124.32	16.00	29.80	2612.00	83.60
Sichuan	8375.00	15.60	34.60	13758.00	164.27
Shaanxi	3876.21	15.10	32.00	750.00	19.35
Tianjin	1561.83	14.40	31.60	620.00	39.70
Hebei	7591.97	14.40	40.80	570.00	7.51
Hunan	6918.38	14.00	31.50	5756.00	83.20
Shanghai	2428.14	13.70	29.90	1780.00	73.31
Beijing	2153.60	13.60	31.70	52.00	2.41
Jilin	2690.73	13.40	24.30	4747.00	176.42
Shandong	10070.21	13.40	34.90	N/A	N/A
Heilongjiang	3751.30	12.90	40.10	3705.00	98.77
Liaoning	4351.70	12.70	27.20	N/A	N/A
Guangdong	11521.00	12.70	34.90	2045.00	17.75
Yunnan	4858.30	12.40	54.50	2650.00	54.55
Jiangxi	4666.10	12.10	46.60	889.00	19.05
Henan	9640.00	12.00	40.10	888.00	9.21
Guangxi	4960.00	11.90	34.80	2467.00	49.74
Qinghai	607.82	11.80	38.50	260.00	42.78
Jiangsu	8070.00	11.50	30.80	5472.00	67.81
Xinjiang	2523.22	11.40	21.70	3269.00	129.56
Zhejiang	5850.00	11.20	32.70	1004.00	17.16
Hubei	5927.00	10.60	42.00	900.00	15.18
Shanxi	3729.22	10.40	34.50	1000.00	26.82
Gansu	2647.43	9.10	36.00	600.00	22.66
Anhui	6365.90	8.50	17.20	315.00	4.95
Ningxia	694.66	8.00	37.90	450.00	64.78
Tibet	350.56	6.50	34.40	N/A	N/A
Guizhou	3622.95	6.20	27.60	3777.00	104.25
Taiwan	2360.31			N/A	N/A

| Hong Kong | 750.07 | N/A | N/A |
| Macau | 67.96 | N/A | N/A |

By comparing these two sets of data, it seems that areas with higher diabetes prevalence also have more psychiatric hospital beds, suggesting a certain correlation between the two. From any perspective, increased survival pressure is a major trigger for the high incidence of various diseases. Chronic illnesses further exacerbate survival pressures, creating a vicious cycle. Under such intense survival pressure, fulfilling higher-level desires is certainly difficult, often leaving people stuck at the basic levels of desires such as food and sex, and sometimes even these cannot be fully satisfied.

23. The Culture of "Guessing"

In the process of societal development, the continuous emergence of new concepts and theories represents a progressive infiltration that disrupts old cultural norms. Due to the difficulty of creating new characters in Chinese, new words are often formed by combining old ones. Consequently, the meanings of these old characters and words, when overlain with new concepts, become increasingly unstable. Theories from earlier periods become harder to understand over time, and what appears to be cultural inheritance on the surface ultimately devolves into confusing and meaningless interpretations and guesses.

Chinese culture can be described as a "guessing" culture. Much of daily communication relies on experience and probabilistic inference to guess others' true intentions. People live according to established conventions, and language nearly loses its pivotal role. The lack of clarity and disorder in expression is ubiquitous, making this language unsuitable for computer analysis. Even humans sometimes struggle to decipher the exact meaning of a Chinese sentence, as it can encompass multiple meanings. Speakers may intentionally do this; the so-called "double entendre" is an effective form of humor both domestically and abroad.

24. "Diaosi" and "Xiaozhi"

The inventors of the term "diaosi" (loser) can be considered cultural ruffians or even cultural hooligans. They took a refined language and turned it vulgar, denigrating a broad segment of the population, and quickly disseminated it through the internet. "Xiaozhi" (petty bourgeois) is the opposite of "diaosi." These two words share the same final syllable in pronunciation, creating a comparative contrast. This phenomenon of creating unsophisticated or internet slang words has an inherent inevitability. Elegant words and concepts have almost been exhausted, making it difficult to find refined words to accurately describe new concepts. As a result, more vulgar and obscure words are used.

The "diaosi" group essentially represents the portion of the population with a relatively low standard of living due to the widening wealth gap in society. In other words, most people live in this state. Those who have entered the petty bourgeois lifestyle look down on the lifestyles of the less privileged, maligning them with vicious words to showcase their superiority. This might force the weaker group to adopt the values and lifestyles of the petty bourgeois. However, the age-old saying "economic base determines the superstructure" is hard to break. The laggards are not allowed by the market environment to quickly advance into the petty bourgeois lifestyle. When a "xiaozhi" and a "diaosi" sit together, they have no common ground. Essentially, there is no market overlap between them—you don't need anything from me, and I can't provide what you want. Human social behavior is fundamentally market exchange behavior. If the market is severely fragmented and certain groups have little interaction, society

will also experience division and segregation.

25. National Destruction Value

We often use the English acronym GDP (Gross Domestic Product) to measure a country's economic development level. It refers to the total monetary value of goods and services created by a nation within a fixed statistical period. The higher the GDP, the higher the total value of goods and services created, and consequently, the higher the standard of living for the people should be.

However, due to some irrational behaviors in our economic activities, such as accidents, illnesses, property damage, and the cycle of demolishing and rebuilding infrastructure, some of our activities are essentially destroying past labor achievements. Fundamentally, these changes in accounting records hide enormous waste, but no department has specifically highlighted and calculated these as separate statistics. They are merely counted as depreciation, medical expenses, and human capital replacement costs, among other things. Here, I will tentatively call this "National Destruction Value," as opposed to "National Consumption Value," to correspond with "Gross Domestic Product." Consumption generates positive utility for people, whereas unnecessary losses and waste do not increase welfare; instead, they increase the labor required for corresponding remedial work.

26. The Frenzy of Tutoring Classes

The phenomenon of widespread tutoring in the education sector, where teachers profit from offering extra classes, is an unreasonable burden on students. When tutoring becomes pervasive, the value of schools and teachers themselves diminishes, leading people to turn to private education institutions. When corruption reaches a certain level, the original system collapses, fragmenting into smaller entities where the "normal" and "abnormal" coexist. Teachers who do not participate in tutoring face lower incomes, resulting in low motivation across the entire educational system. In response, the government might raise teachers' salaries, ideally to a level not lower than civil servants. However, the burden ultimately falls on the public, as increasing teachers' wages means taxpayers have to foot the bill. Education does not directly produce anything and its benefits are slow to materialize. Consequently, the illicit practice of tutoring persists, and taxpayers suffer from having to invest in both off-campus tutoring and paying taxes to support well-paid teachers, effectively expanding the investment in education.

As a result, many may find it more lucrative to become a teacher rather than pursuing other careers. This creates a "self-circulating" cycle in education where even top graduates from prestigious universities like Tsinghua or Peking University end up returning to the education system as teachers rather than engaging in more socially beneficial research or corporate roles. Overall, this reduces the output of education, as the education system continuously expands

its self-circulation, extracting more and more resources from society.

27. The Rampancy of Prostitution

The prostitution industry can be seen as a last resort for women. Women are naturally more vulnerable, often unable to do heavy physical labor, and if they experience failures in marriage or career, they can find themselves in a very dire situation. If they are not allowed to sell sexual services, low-educated women who cannot find formal employment have no choice but to rely on social welfare. However, social welfare in China seems to be nearly invisible; while everyone knows it exists, it is hard to find, and people often avoid it due to issues of "face," preferring to engage in the gray market instead.

Given that the number of offspring one can raise in a limited lifespan is finite, for most people, raising one or two children is already very difficult. Thus, over a long life, much of the sex that does not result in offspring is considered "ineffective." It only satisfies the brain's innate drive for reproduction. If sexual function is not used for a long time, it may decline. The relationship between a client and a prostitute is, in essence, a fleeting form of love, but it usually does not lead to any lasting results. One party provides material compensation, and the other offers services. In this sense, premarital sex is not much different from prostitution. Prostitution can also bring incurable sexually transmitted diseases. Using condoms, however, is not considered true sexual behavior since the sexual organs do not make complete "contact."

Engaging in prostitution after marriage is an act of infidelity, potentially causing cross-infection of sexually transmitted diseases and hiding the seeds of betrayal, which may foretell the breakdown of the family.

28. The Rampancy of Fraud

China's vast territory and large population make it fertile ground for various fraud cases. It's not just fraud; even many murder cases are challenging to solve, with some criminals managing to stay hidden for ten to twenty years. The primary reason is that these criminals can move across cities and provinces, making joint capture efforts difficult due to jurisdictional divisions among police forces. This difficulty arises from issues of public resource allocation: if a criminal from area A flees to area B, it consumes B's police resources to capture them. If A's police are deployed to B, it requires more resources to support such operations. Fraud cases are particularly tricky because the perpetrators often operate from different locations, leading to complex issues of evidence collection and inter-jurisdictional cooperation.

In actual economic activities, interregional interactions are unavoidable, which can lead to many disputes. Gradually, some people noticed the loopholes in these interactions and developed them into profitable scams. Suppose a fraudster invests 2,000 yuan to scam 1,000 people and one person falls for it, yielding 20,000 yuan; this results in a tenfold return, with minimal risk of getting caught. Given the high return on such low-risk endeavors, many individuals are tempted to take the plunge, leading to a high incidence of fraud cases.

There was once a report by state media about a shocking fraud case where a Beijing woman was scammed into selling her property worth over 5 million yuan under the pretense of a prosecutorial investigation. The entire transaction was

completed in less than three days.

29. The Dilemma of Cultural Export

The United States exports its culture through blockbuster movies, Apple-brand electronic products, video games, TV series, and American values. These cultural products generate substantial international revenue. In contrast, Chinese culture seems only acceptable to the Chinese. Due to prevalent illogical elements and the non-correspondence between Chinese and English translations, foreign audiences often struggle to grasp the ideas expressed in Chinese cultural products. Moreover, Chinese cultural products may lack deep ideological content. Domestic ideological censorship and constraints make it challenging to find themes worth exploring, leading to art gradually disconnecting from real life and creating a surreal absurdity. Such an unhealthy cultural ecosystem is difficult for foreigners to accept. Consequently, in international trade exchanges, the lack of cultural product exports forces China to rely on material product exports to maintain economic balance.

Additionally, the instability of the domestic language environment has led to many misinterpretations in the translations of foreign works. Some non-professionals like to spread non-standard language on the internet, further complicating the ability of domestic audiences with limited discernment skills to accurately understand foreign ideas and cultures. This exacerbates the disconnection between the domestic cultural environment and the global stage, leading to the creation of distorted cultural products.

As a result, China has to earn foreign exchange by enhancing domestic manufacturing, building infrastructure abroad, and exporting labor—methods lacking intellectual property rights. In the long run, the balance of payments must be maintained because the foreign exchange earned will eventually be spent. If one only earns without spending, what is the point of earning? One adverse effect of this is that massive manufacturing leads to significant resource consumption and environmental pollution domestically, putting pressure on the ecological environment and negatively impacting public health.

III. Political Life

Humans are political animals. They use language to communicate and establish rules to replace violent conflicts over interests. But what kind of political situation would arise if they used a flawed tool for communication?

1. No Way to Give a Speech

In China, it seems that public political speeches do not exist. Such large gatherings require various security measures and coordination, which seem impractical for citizens of a developing country focused on making a living. In institutions like schools, speeches are usually limited to praising the main themes of the state, and are not suitable for proposing deeper political ideas. These kinds of speeches are neither accepted nor allowed. Given the dominance of the ruling party, it is almost impossible for an independent political organization with widespread support to emerge. This effectively isolates most ordinary people from participating in politics. To pursue a political career, one must join the existing party organization and operate within the permitted framework.

Dissenting opinions are suppressed and cannot be openly expressed. Whether an official uses the official language or the local dialect during a speech is often inappropriate. To enter politics, one must use the officially mandated standard language, but everyday communication among the people resists official jargon because it is "inconvenient." Essentially, people's thinking language remains their dialect. Many dialect terms are either rarely used in the official language or lack corresponding definitions. When expressing ideas in the official language, people must mentally translate from their dialect, creating various "translation" barriers similar to those encountered when translating foreign words.

Officials habitually use the local dialect in daily interactions with the public but must use the official language in formal settings like meetings. This gradually creates a psychological effect where the official language represents the elevated status of officials, while the dialect represents the lower status of common people. The language one speaks thus signifies one's identity and status. This linguistic hierarchy might be common in colonies, but it is strange to see it within a single ethnic group.

When speaking the official language to common people, an official is distancing themselves and assuming an authoritative stance; when speaking the dialect, they are getting closer to the people and temporarily "forgetting" their official role. This puts Chinese officials at all levels in a perpetually uncomfortable position.

2. Drinking Culture

The Chinese are an intriguing people. Baijiu, a liquor that is both unpleasant to drink and harmful to the body, is a must-have beverage at gatherings. This bitter, foul-smelling liquid is not only devoid of any enjoyable taste, but it also burns the throat and stomach, and damages the liver and kidneys. Chinese drinking culture resembles a gang initiation ritual—before being accepted, you must endure considerable discomfort to prove your loyalty and gain the trust of existing members. Members hope that you will be willing to help and keep secrets in the future.

At the table, the etiquette is hierarchical, reflecting status and familiarity. When toasting, one's glass must not be higher than that of a superior. When offering a toast to a leader, one must nod and bow to show respect. Failing to understand these customs indicates that you do not grasp the rules, suggesting that in future collaborations, you may not act according to others' expectations. Consequently, you may not be invited to the next gathering and might face difficulties at work. Colleagues may adopt a strict attitude towards you, making things difficult in situations where leniency could have been applied, enforcing minor rules to cause you trouble. This would eventually force you to either comply or leave.

A small glass of liquor can significantly impact your career, highlighting how harsh the living conditions are in China, where even trivial matters can be a matter of life and death. It is no wonder that the Chinese have struggled to develop a refined culture. If your existence is as uncertain as a death row inmate's, with execution looming unpredictably, you would hardly be inclined to engage in profound studies. Instead, you would constantly amass wealth to guard against potential betrayals. This is the reality of survival in China.

3. Criminal Underworld

The criminal underworld is also a part of society and represents a form of local self-governance, albeit unrecognized by the central authorities and, consequently, by the law. These organizations often employ unethical methods to exploit the people, making them a societal cancer. Ordinary citizens have to support the top-level government, the grassroots government, and the criminal organizations. Surviving under such immense pressure is a miracle in itself. Since the central authorities often appear to neglect the grassroots level, local governments and criminal groups naturally form a more robust coalition, gradually establishing a leadership core, resulting in a "local emperor." The primary objective of such organizations is to engage in highly profitable illegal activities. Their inherent drive for personal gain is also essential for the organization's survival.

Although the central government is distant, it does not remain entirely indifferent. When things escalate to a certain point, causing widespread public dissatisfaction and threatening the central authority's credibility, a crackdown on organized crime becomes necessary. Shockingly, in some regions, long-standing crime bosses have held positions like police chief.

4. Politics Under Dialects

The Chinese language itself reflects the characteristics of Chinese politics: inconsistent rules. Each region has its own unique dialect features, and many words are used differently. It is very difficult for outsiders to integrate into the local dialect system. This makes the top-level government's management of the grassroots essentially disconnected: no one likes to listen to outsiders. While outwardly maintaining recognition of the central authority, people actually still protect local interests. Although they live in urban areas, their culture remains that of farmers. You can't leave, and others can't come in.

Due to the numerous ambiguities and errors in Chinese, there is a trap of low-level repetition in culture and national spirit. Any advanced emotions cannot be properly expressed in daily life; civilization only exists on television and in classrooms. If people want to discuss a relatively advanced policy issue, many obstacles and misunderstandings arise. This makes a democratic system based on speeches and elections unworkable. Discussions are often chaotic and unclear. To ensure efficiency, people can only choose familiar tasks to perform. Attempting to implement changes is extremely difficult due to the aforementioned "pollution" effect. The difficulty of creating new vocabulary makes it impossible for any novel ideas to spread smoothly, and errors increase with distance. The interpretation of issues ultimately falls to whoever has more brute force, reverting to the logic of tyranny and despotism.

The final result is the formation of a stable autocratic power structure. Although not very fair, it at least maintains some efficiency. The oppressed can only hope for a "good emperor" to sympathize with the people's suffering, and the only feasible way is through bribery. This allows those in power to spare a bit of attention to help you in their busy schedules. The saying "If you want to get rich, scrape off everyone's heads" encapsulates how grand corruption gradually accumulates over time. This is the inherent logic of the Chinese political structure.

5. Why Foreign Monks are Good at Chanting Scriptures

A foreign monk, first and foremost, shares the same faith as local monks. Monasteries in various places can be seen as branches of a chain store, operating under the same brand. A foreign monk may have held a certain status in his original "branch" and did relatively well, which is why he was sent to exchange experiences. Even if things don't go well for him here, he has a fallback option to return home and continue his life. If he gets unhappy, he might leave at any time, without causing any substantial impact on the local power hierarchy. Thus, even if there are issues with how he chants the scriptures, people won't hold it against him too much.

We often see "seconded" officials who may not hold real power in a new place. They are sent by higher-ups to learn management experiences and get a taste of life elsewhere. These officials are like foreign monks, and they are likely to be promoted upon returning. For such officials, people generally greet them with smiles and don't engage deeply. They also don't entrust them with significant local matters, making the life of these foreign monks quite comfortable.

6. Women's Advantage in Expression

Men are naturally less skilled in verbal expression compared to women. Given that Chinese is a complex and chaotic language, this creates a significant problem for Chinese men. The language system, which represents a patriarchal society, ironically suits women better, presenting substantial obstacles for the primary power holders — men. This results in the peculiar phenomenon of eloquent female leaders emerging in positions that require strong speaking abilities.

The reason men struggle with Chinese expression is due to their brains being more logical, while Chinese is a language characterized by chaotic and illogical rules. Finding an appropriate way to express oneself becomes extremely difficult. In contrast, women's brains are more adaptable to existing language rules and less focused on logic, so they face fewer obstacles in expression. When you hear a woman on the radio or TV fluently talking but with no substantial insights, you might think the world is truly doomed. Therefore, the author argues that Chinese inherently has a feminine quality—not only in its tonal system but also in its pronunciation, where sounds are often mixed and squeezed out almost simultaneously. Speaking clearly requires significant control.

When non-logical yet incessantly verbose women gain power, the disastrous consequences can be unimaginable. Recently, there was news about a female discipline inspection commissioner who was killed and her body discarded.

Women seem to adapt well to the many drawbacks of Chinese because they naturally do not emphasize logic and dialectics. Have you ever heard of a female philosopher? This lack of logical emphasis ironically becomes an advantage, fitting well into the Chinese linguistic environment. Thus, while women may not leave behind profound theoretical legacies, they often play the role of spokespersons in contemporary life.

Disasters often brew in these peculiar places. When illogical yet pervasive notions dominate, they inevitably clash with the harsh realities of the world. However, human social activities do not always adhere to universal physical laws. A widely accepted mistake can work in certain contexts for a short time, but its hidden dangers are immense. When this irrational logic reaches its boundaries, irreconcilable contradictions arise. Natural laws do not bend to human will, and erroneous theories will ultimately encounter insurmountable gaps in reality.

7. Complete Equality Does Not Exist

Everyone is likely familiar with the story of how introducing wolves into American parks improved the survival conditions of deer. Excessive stress can shorten lifespans, but having no stress at all can lead to physical decline, which also shortens lifespans.

A top-performing male student might not be attractive and won't be as popular with girls as a mischievous, handsome boy. A tall basketball player might have very low scientific knowledge. A famous actor might have little status at home, bearing various obligations. The world is a diverse place, and pressures exist on all levels; sometimes, pressure itself is the driving force for survival.

Therefore, complete equality is almost impossible. Making everyone identical, like hydrogen atoms, is extremely difficult. Differences naturally and inevitably arise in subtle ways, beyond any human control. What people can do is to develop individual differences that benefit the group while limiting those that are harmful.

8. Who Do Beautiful Women Choose

In any nation, beautiful women are a scarce resource. Defining beauty is a profoundly philosophical question. From a cultural and psychological perspective, a beautiful woman's facial features have aesthetic appeal. This appeal might stem from the human brain's assessment of the potential survival resources her appearance represents. Throughout human history, people have developed stable likes and dislikes about various things, and one's facial expression reflects these feelings. A beautiful woman's facial expressions tend to display more joy, or her facial features naturally align in a way that suggests a favorable living environment and more positive emotions. In contrast, the facial proportions of a less attractive woman might resemble expressions of displeasure, evoking negative associations.

Moreover, a beautiful woman's physique symbolizes better physical health and reproductive capabilities, stronger immune and endocrine systems, longer life expectancy, higher cultural literacy, and access to more social resources. Ordinary women may lack some of these traits.

Beautiful women are more inclined to prefer men with abundant social resources. In China's oligarchic political structure, resources are excessively concentrated among a few in power. Consequently, those in power naturally attract many beautiful women. Leaders are typically individuals with extensive social skills. Thus, those with broad social abilities gain more optimal reproductive resources, passing on these traits to their descendants and perpetuating this pattern. The Chinese saying, "A good man has no good wife, while a bad man has a pretty wife," reflects this reality.

Human civilization advances through the gradual accumulation of knowledge by dedicated researchers, not through opportunistic politicians. If this marriage logic continues to evolve, where diligent researchers lack marital happiness, and the offspring of cunning individuals become increasingly attractive, one might question the future prospects of such a society.

9. The Debate on Good and Evil

If the standard for distinguishing between good and bad people is based on their approach to the distribution of benefits and their distortion of fairness and justice, then ultimately, good people are those who suffer losses, while bad people are those who take advantage. If this imbalance is not corrected, it will lead to many negative consequences. Good people might suddenly turn bad to change the situation and ironically become the bad ones. Trying to educate bad people to be as morally upright as good people is nearly impossible because their upbringing and living environment have ingrained their behaviors.

Being bad is almost innate; it's in their bones. Making them behave like good people makes them uncomfortable. In their view, good people are hypocritical bad people who only disguise themselves to gain greater benefits. Bad people perceive the good behavior of others as a nauseating pretense, a violation of human nature. "The world runs for profit." Every person's existence requires a certain benefit foundation. Hidden schemes are almost inevitable, as they are a rational choice and an unshakeable equilibrium solution in game theory. To bad people, occasional altruism is merely an insignificant act in front of others. Therefore, to avoid being seen as pretentious, truly good people should do good deeds anonymously.

This creates an effect where good deeds go unrecognized because only selfless acts are considered genuinely good. Doing good deeds should then be done without leaving a name, even keeping the deeds themselves in the dark. Who in the world has no personal interests? Legitimate personal interests are the foundation of one's existence and cannot be compromised. If legitimate personal interests can be abandoned, imposing this standard on others would be a great evil. If one cannot gain a heavenly afterlife through religion, there is little reason for people to be genuinely good in this life, as it contradicts their own existence. Moreover, the ubiquitous competitive relationships between people often mean that the downfall of others can be beneficial. This is the result of competitive pressure.

10. Compliance or Cheating

The world is full of prisoner's dilemmas, where cooperation or betrayal is a difficult choice. If you choose to cooperate and the other party chooses to cheat, you will pay a heavy price. Although mutual cooperation is beneficial for everyone, you cannot bear the risk of the other party cheating, so the final result is that everyone chooses to cheat.

Marriage, too, is like a prisoner's dilemma. On one hand, people want to cooperate, but they cannot resist the temptation to cheat or the cost of being betrayed, so rational choices often lean towards betrayal. Infidelity is common, and once discovered, it marks a significant loss for one party, leading to the breakdown of the cooperative relationship and a return to single status. If marriage is based solely on sexual relations, betrayal is almost inevitable. The purpose of a stable family relationship is nearly to facilitate and worry-free infidelity. This all boils down to costs: on one hand, we want stable families, on the other, we desire more sexual partners. Under such a crisis, the only solution is to increase the cost of establishing a family and the price of its dissolution to deter cheaters. The metaphorical Sword of Damocles hanging over everyone's head is the secret to maintaining stable relationships. However, this can backfire, with the weaker party possibly enduring the consequences of divorce and being oppressed by the other party. Naturally, one can resort to legal measures to protect their interests, with divorce lawsuits being the most common.

Similarly, a bureaucratic government department has this characteristic. Establishing and maintaining a government institution requires a significant time investment. Building a satisfactory government is a complex systemic issue. Once established, changing its personnel and structure is difficult. This is where cheating begins. Officials and the public are like a marital relationship; corruption and embezzlement are almost inevitable. A stable and rigid government department is almost certainly designed for corruption, mainly to facilitate officials in exploiting the public. A rigid government department can almost be 100% identified as corrupt. If people tolerate corruption, officials should have their salaries canceled and let them support themselves through corruption, as this is a right granted by the system. Corruption in China is a culture, a system recognized by the public. Some gain greater benefits by bribing officials, forming an interest group with them, while law-abiding citizens are rejected everywhere and eventually forced to give in. Instead of futilely resisting such a cultural environment, one might join the mass of people benefiting from bribery, finding immediate relief and pleasure. Few can resist this temptation. Compared to the dream of uniting the majority, joining a small interest group is more realistic. Only when this gradual change leads to a qualitative change, when small interest groups become too large and the exploited group has almost no resources left, will this structure become unstable and possibly restrained. By then, corrupt officials might have accumulated billions. You either exploit others or be exploited; if you resist, you might become like those you detest, "living as the person you hate." There are no strictly good or bad people; phenomena arise from rational games everyone plays.

What impact does this exploitation have? Through bribery and corruption, benefits are transferred to places and people where they shouldn't go. This is like cancer in a living organism, continually absorbing nutrients without producing useful functions, suppressing the metabolism of normal tissues. Eventually, in its late stages, it becomes incurable. However, a nation is not indivisible like a human body. People can resort to revolutionary movements to separate the necrotic parts, while legal means in a civilized society are a painstaking and lengthy process. For a short life, dealing with these issues can waste much time that could be spent enjoying life, which seems so unworthy.

Corruption is a culture, a necessary result of China's social structure. Due to China's regional cultural characteristics, the free movement of people becomes extremely difficult. People prefer familiar things because they require no additional learning costs and seem safe and risk-free on the surface. This is the fundamental reason for the stagnation of Chinese society. When an outsider comes to work in a new environment, they must handle at least three languages: their hometown dialect, the local dialect, and Mandarin (which also divides into spoken and written forms). No wonder many Chinese are not good at expression; with such a chaotic linguistic environment, it's very difficult to speak well. If you can't speak clearly, how can you engage in other social activities? The difficulty in the free movement of people means that resources, centered around people, naturally adhere to the principle of "fertile water does not flow to others' fields." This internal logic severely conflicts with the free exchange of market economies.

If good things are not given to outsiders, outsiders' good things won't come in either. People hold on to their little plots of land without exchange or possibility of exchange. Adding English to this multi-language system would cause even greater confusion and difficulty in communication, making it harder for ordinary people to adapt. Therefore, most parts of China can hardly achieve true openness to the outside world.

11. Corrupt Officials as Local Lords

An interesting phenomenon in China is that many of the officials caught and punished for corruption are deputies rather than principal officials. The reason likely lies in the fact that deputies usually serve in local positions for extended periods, gradually forming stable networks of relationships and interest groups. Over time, these officials develop a mutual understanding and cooperation with their local networks. To some extent, local officials become interest communities with a coordinating core, which grants these individuals the power and influence akin to regional "lords" within their jurisdictions. The saying "officials protect each other" holds true; once an investigation starts from the top, it often results in a "domino effect," affecting many people and causing a significant local political upheaval. A common phrase is, "If you' re not a good official, you might end up in prison." Usually, unless corruption has become severe, officials are not rigorously investigated.

Principal officials, however, are quite special. Typically, they are appointed by higher authorities and rotate after a few years, making it difficult for them to develop long-term relationships in any one place. Principal officials are like imperial envoys with high authority, overseeing and managing local affairs. It's challenging for them to quickly integrate with local interest groups. Building relationships requires significant investment, such as working together on numerous projects, sharing many ideas, and especially organizing many social dinners. Social dinners often involve drinking, which can harm health. Who would sacrifice their health to build a network that cannot be sustained long-term? Ultimately, such efforts might be in vain. On the surface, the frequent rotation of top officials by higher authorities is intended to prevent the formation of "local lords." The power structure emphasizes the absolute leadership of principal officials, but it is the deputies who primarily manage local politics. To prevent excessive concentration of power, multiple deputy positions are often established within various departments. After prolonged competition, similar outcomes often emerge across regions, where multiple deputies form a coalition to share interests, creating an implicit understanding of governance.

IV. Interesting Questions

While we are diligently working, we must occasionally look up to see the road ahead. The author believes that by exploring some profound philosophical questions, we might be able to find a way out of our current predicaments.

1. Algorithms and Artificial Intelligence

Intelligence and technology are discoveries of pre-existing natural laws by humans, rather than inventions, including theories like relativity. Algorithms and artificial intelligence (AI) merely clarify, standardize, and mathematize the inherent logic of things, ultimately mastering this internal logic. AI will eventually design marvels that closely mimic natural biological characteristics, iterating and evolving rapidly to create highly efficient frameworks that will help humanity govern the universe's resources. The future of humanity will extend into the vast, limitless cosmos.

AI cannot comprehend human emotions because it lacks human sensory organs. These emotions are relative, "living" things that change with the environment. Unless AI can dynamically adjust its "subjective" feelings in real-time according to environmental changes and respond accordingly — so-called "adaptive responses"—it can only be said to possess initial human-like intelligence.

In reality, machine intelligence is fundamentally different from human intelligence. When solving a problem, a machine follows a predetermined method and will continue to do so indefinitely. If it encounters an obstacle, it won't proactively avoid it or devise an alternative method unless such methods are also predefined. A machine's most significant feature is its near-infallibility and lack of emotions.

Humans, in contrast, possess foresight and imagination. If one method fails, humans will think of alternative solutions. Repetitive and monotonous tasks lead to boredom, while success in tasks results in emotional highs, sometimes causing extreme behavior. Humans frequently make mistakes, regardless of the simplicity of a task, with complex problems being even more error-prone. This is why humans are said to have "bounded rationality"—it's challenging for humans to consider every aspect comprehensively. However, humans are also imaginative, capable of abstract thinking and creating knowledge, leading to continuous progress.

Machines and the human brain differ fundamentally. To create a machine with the same functions as the human brain might require building a machine brain that simulates the human brain, a task of immense complexity with uncertain feasibility. If, one day, a man-made machine brain possesses all the functionalities of the human brain with fewer errors, the human brain might then be regarded as an inferior machine by comparison.

2. Why Music is Pleasant

Why music is pleasant is another profound philosophical question. If human activities can be understood as evaluations of resource acquisition abilities, then the beauty of music can be seen in the richness of its melody. The brain continuously identifies the pattern of changes in pitch; the richer the pattern, the more information it seems to contain. In human society, rich information often represents more resources or hints at more ways to acquire them. Therefore, a symphony is considered more musical than a solo erhu performance, a choir is richer than a solo, and a multi-instrument ensemble is grander than a single-instrument performance. The climax of a song abstractly summarizes the various pieces of information conveyed earlier.

Noise, on the other hand, lacks any identifiable meaningful pattern. It represents death and wasted life, simple mechanical repetition devoid of any beneficial information, making it unpleasant to hear.

3. Sex and Immunity

Sex is the process through which humans recombine genes. Male and female individuals each contribute half of their genes, repairing and combining them to form a new individual. This process allows genes to be updated and transmitted, avoiding gradual degradation and breakdown. The pleasure derived from sexual activity comes from the stimulation of the brain by various sensory organs and immune system responses. A series of invasive sexual behaviors helps sperm penetrate the immune barriers of the reproductive organs, leading to fertilization with the egg.

If the immune system is too strong, it can lead to infertility issues, reducing the chances of conception. Conversely, if the immune system is too weak, it can result in reproductive organ diseases, affecting the viability of sperm and eggs, making conception equally difficult. Therefore, one could argue that pleasurable sex indicates an individual with a well-balanced immune system. The immune systems of the mating partners are balanced and healthy, and this characteristic is passed on through their genes.

4. American Democracy

We know that the United States has been established for over 200 years and has developed a relatively stable and mature political system. The two major parties, the Democratic Party and the Republican Party, continually stage election dramas. The citizens vote based on their approval of the candidates' platforms and character, with additional support measures like the representative system. As an outsider, my understanding is limited to this, having never been abroad or lived in another country, but I've gained some insight from Gao Xiaosong's talk show "Xiaoshuo."

If the prosperity and advancement of the U.S. are due to the superiority of its system, can we Chinese adopt it wholesale? I think the possibility is very slim.

Campaigning requires money, and no one would spend money on something without returns. How could our vast population establish a grassroots system to support elections? Currently, China's per capita GDP is around $10,000. Organizing large-scale campaigns and elections would require enormous time and financial resources. If each voter spends ten hours per round understanding the candidates, the total time spent by 1.4 billion people would be about 14 billion hours. This is an enormous economic figure. If we invested this time and money elsewhere, it might yield more economic benefits.

Additionally, we must consider whether the election results would generate greater societal benefits. Clearly, electing a leader every four years is too costly for the Chinese. A ten-year cycle might be more affordable. The U.S. essentially has an eight-year cycle, with relatively low competition pressure during mid-term elections. With a population of over 300 million and a per capita GDP about three times ours, their total economic output is similar to ours, but their per capita spending is much higher. Though elections are expensive, the cost relative to their total income is low, so Americans can afford this "game," while we cannot.

Currently, we oppose bourgeois liberalization, and elections are a product of such liberalization. The bourgeoisie can use their financial power to support a candidate. If successful, they gain substantial political returns. If they fail, their considerable wealth allows them to continue betting on future elections. Examples of ordinary people successfully funding their campaigns are increasingly rare. Major corporations, through control of social networks and media advertising, dominate the public opinion market with overwhelming advantages. Without money, it's difficult to expand influence because you can't use societal resources on a large scale for free.

5. Utility Integration

No matter what we do, even if it starts off feeling enjoyable, we will eventually grow weary of it. Our brain instinctively prevents us from continuously engaging in one activity. If we liken the pleasure derived from activities to digging in the ground, then repeatedly doing the same thing is like digging a tunnel in a straight line. As the tunnel gets deeper and longer, extracting more dirt becomes increasingly difficult, reducing the total pleasure that can be obtained within a limited time. To maximize pleasure, we need to switch directions and engage in different pleasurable activities, akin to changing the digging direction to increase efficiency. However, as the pit grows larger, both changing directions and continuing to dig in the same place become progressively harder, and our psychological age advances, making it difficult to find interest in many things.

Thus, the total utility one gains in life is comparable to the total amount of dirt dug up, approximating a spherical shape. Some specialists might dig a long tunnel in a particular field, requiring much more effort than the average person. While a two-dimensional perspective could suffice, I use a three-dimensional image to calculate utility because different fields may overlap and correlate, making it impossible to view them in isolation. Digging in one direction might also touch upon adjacent areas, yielding unexpected benefits.

Therefore, the total utility a person can achieve is a three-dimensional integral bounded by their depth of exploration in various fields. This is why we cultivate broad interests, as it can expand our total gains and allow us to derive more benefits in a finite lifetime.

Those who continuously delve into a specific field are also happy because their talents compensate for the decreasing efficiency of gaining utility as the tunnel deepens, providing them with additional motivation and leading to achievements beyond the average person. When encountering bottlenecks in deep exploration, talent becomes a crucial differentiator, allowing geniuses to stand out. Talent likely involves innate factors and specialized brain development through nurturing, giving some people an intuitive understanding of specific fields. This intuition processes complex tasks rapidly, often without the person being consciously aware of it. Analyzing a genius's thought process requires slowing down and breaking it into many steps, a challenging task for current brain research. We can only approximate optimal solutions by experimenting with various algorithms.

6. Interstellar Resources

With the advancement of mathematical theories related to "Ricci flow," humanity will eventually master black holes, spacetime, stellar energy, and planetary resources. These resources are virtually limitless for humanity. No longer will we be confined to the tiny speck of cosmic dust that is Earth. When we possess nearly infinite energy and materials, our ability to transform the world will be greatly enhanced. We will be able to manufacture elements, synthesize water, metals, and more. We will undertake engineering projects on a cosmic scale. If we fail to utilize the entire universe to expand human living space, it would be an immense waste.

7. Longevity

Human thought arises from history, culture, and individual processing. Essentially, humans are products of their communities. The existence of a person relies on the existence of their nation. If a nation's culture disappears, even if some genes continue in mixed-race descendants, their influence will be negligible due to assimilation. Thus, no matter how long an individual's lifespan, they are merely one of many individuals within their nation—a replica or a clone, albeit not an identical one, always having some unique traits and differences.

The global environment and cultures are constantly changing. A person with an exceptionally long life would still be unable to traverse the entirety of history. If their primary concerns are no longer disease and aging, they must then focus on adapting to a changing world. At some point, they may find that the troubles they must address far outweigh the pleasures they can enjoy, and no one would likely relish such a life.

Therefore, a nation is the primary form of human existence; individual importance is relatively minor. Even individuals who hold special places in history are products of their nation's cultural identity. If this cultural identity changes, evaluations of historical figures will also shift. For example, a skilled hunter who saved his tribe might be a legendary figure in that tribe's history, yet appear trivial or laughable to outsiders.

8. AI Government to End Corruption

Corrupt politicians are almost an unsolvable problem. Seeking protection through bribery is the equilibrium solution in the "prisoner's dilemma" among those without power. One method to escape this dilemma is migration, but for Chinese people, migration involves overcoming numerous obstacles, including adapting to different terrains, climates, dialects, and foods. Therefore, it's very difficult for Chinese people to escape this "prisoner's dilemma."

When quantum computing and intelligent algorithms combine, can we create an intelligent brain to handle various social management issues? A government no longer operated by greedy and cowardly humans — machines don't take bribes. They only execute outcomes according to pre-set rules, which can be established by the public through a fair process. The actual implementation would be carried out by robots because if humans were involved in any stage of the process, corruption could arise. If humans are managed entirely by intelligent machines, it's uncertain whether escaping the old chains will lead to new ones.

9. "Flow" and "Field"

Physical laws have been studied very deeply, from Newton to Einstein, and the recent detection of gravitational waves. These developments seem to point to one conclusion: the universe is a product of the entanglement between time, space, and matter, influenced by each other. However, we have not yet fully understood these relationships or how to control matter and space themselves while ensuring the stability and continuity of time.

What we do know is that, besides the universe itself, there doesn't seem to exist any completely self-sufficient, closed system. If all entities interact with each other, this breaks the definition of matter itself. Everything is merely a temporary manifestation, a part of a system interacting with other parts, and distinguishing between them is just a necessary approach for humans to discuss specific problems at specific times and places. If nothing can be self-sufficient, then no object is isolated, thus breaking the definition of any single thing and infinitely extending outward. So, is the entire universe a self-sufficient system? The universe is continuously expanding with no apparent boundaries, suggesting that this dynamic motion maintains a temporary state of self-sufficiency, preventing its collapse.

Once an event establishes a fixed pattern of movement, recording its trajectory reveals that other influencing factors emerge to disrupt this internal closure. For example, the motion of electrons generates a magnetic field that affects surrounding matter; the flow of water or blood transports substances, creating material accumulation with distinct characteristics along their paths. This flow of matter is common in the human body and significantly affects health. Can we regulate human health by maintaining certain patterns of this material flow?

Human daily activities can also be viewed as a flow. If we frequently experience injuries, the body makes "adaptive changes." Here, I want to introduce an imprecise concept called the externality of flow. Every event occurring in a time slice results in an adaptive outcome in the overall time flow, which might be called a "time flow field." According to the latest theories, matter might have an external field, determining its state based on the surrounding matter. The next major breakthrough in theory, following Einstein's "relativity of space-time," could be the "relativity of matter."

10. The Essence of Probability

All particles are results of quantum computations in different relative states, following a certain probability distribution. But why does probability arise? It may stem from a natural mathematical distribution that has existed since the emergence of natural numbers. Essentially, this probability might be the ultimate outcome of the relative interactions between all particles, where each event is a form of game theory. These games occur at a quantum level. The overarching principle of these interactions might be to "produce the greatest practical effect with the least energy consumption."

In the interplay between "energy consumption" and practical "effect," all particles engage in a "supra-temporal" game, reacting almost instantaneously. It's as if the behavior of all particles is coordinated by a super quantum computer, producing outcomes in unison. If this is the case, then everything is interconnected instantaneously, and "quantum entanglement" might exist among all matter. Since neither side in a competition can always win or always lose, the quantum computer—or "absolute will"—seems to prefer maintaining a dynamic balance of wins and losses, ensuring the overall stability of the universe. This could be the fundamental rule of our world.

Applying this concept to human activities, we see that while some people achieve great success, many lead ordinary lives. In the repeated competition for social resources, a "normal distribution" phenomenon arises, where very few are exceptionally good or exceptionally poor, and most are at an intermediate level. According to the "fractal" principle, where the whole and its parts have a certain similarity, the probability phenomena observed in socio-economic activities might suggest that similar "game" principles exist at the micro-particle level, warranting further research.

11. Conjecture on Black Holes and the Universe's Boundary

Mathematically, a point's beginning and end is itself, a line segment's boundary is a point, a two-dimensional figure's boundary is a line, and a three-dimensional object's boundary is a surface. However, the universe we live in is not a three-dimensional object, as you cannot place one three-dimensional object inside another in a way that they overlap. This phenomenon, often seen in video games as "clipping" or "wall-hacking," is not permissible in reality. To accommodate all three-dimensional objects, the universe might be a higher-dimensional "Ricci flow," with its boundary being a three-dimensional object. Among the celestial bodies in the universe, only one type has such a nature: the black hole.

Therefore, I conjecture that black holes are the boundaries of the universe. A black hole has no internal part; its "inside" is the "outside" of the universe. Discussing the interior of a black hole is equivalent to discussing the exterior of the universe, which is meaningless. The interior of a black hole does not refer to the inside of its event horizon. Once matter crosses the event horizon, it is transformed by the black hole into fundamental particles and returned to the universe. Matter does not fall into the singularity at the center of the black hole or into an "outside" of the universe, because there is no such "outside." The universe is "existence," and discussing an outside to the universe is akin to discussing the opposite of existence, which is pure "non-existence."

Black holes are just the boundary conditions of a higher-dimensional universe observed from our three-dimensional perspective. The shape and size of a three-dimensional object's boundary determine its size, and similarly, the number, mass, and distribution of black holes determine the universe's expansion state. The universe's expansion and contraction depend on the number and mass of black holes. Since black holes form, "evaporate," and merge, the universe might not expand forever and could contract. According to Hawking's black hole evaporation theory, large black holes evaporate so slowly that it takes the universe's entire lifetime to complete. This implies that the evaporation process may never truly complete. Unless a black hole is very small, its surface area is too small relative to the material it absorbs, which eventually breaches the event horizon, resembling a high tower that bridges the gap between the black hole and spacetime, smoothing out the singularity.

Ultimately, the universe might merge into one very large black hole. The accumulation of matter near the black hole's "event horizon" becomes so dense that it removes entropy, resetting the universe's lifespan and forming a cyclical process. Thus, I conclude that the universe will not end; it will simply restart. However, causally, the restarted universe has almost no connection to its predecessor. This cycle of expansion and contraction severs causal chains, making concepts like "reincarnation" or "transmigration" nearly negligible. People are 99.5% similar, with very little difference. Emphasizing reincarnation suggests that the 0.5% difference outweighs the 99.5% similarity, which is quite mystical.

All things and history return to their origin in the grand rebound, akin to formatting a hard drive. The universe is existence itself, and knowing this provides some comfort. Perhaps the purpose of this world's existence is to give us a bit of sensory stimulation.

12. Steady-State Systems in Nature

If a "self-circulating" phenomenon as described above occurs, it would result in a continuously reinforcing "self-feedback" effect, causing the system to expand until it collapses. However, neither natural ecosystems nor socio-economic systems allow such systems to exist. A system with continuous "positive feedback" will keep expanding until limiting factors become dominant. Conversely, a system with continuous "negative feedback" will continuously shrink and weaken.

Within the human body, many such systems exist where positive and negative feedback mechanisms mutually constrain each other to ensure that various biochemical reactions proceed stably, preventing the collapse of any subsystems that could lead to overall death. This principle applies to all "living" systems. As long as it is a continuously operating system involving living beings, there will always be these two types of feedback mechanisms to regulate and maintain balance.

13. The Purpose of This Era

Society is developing so rapidly that events from yesterday quickly lose their temporal value and are swiftly forgotten as new events flood in. We constantly set new goals, yet we rarely see them through to completion. This is fundamentally a balance between utility and cost. When we achieve a task halfway, we often realize that it does not significantly improve our lives; its utility does not notably increase. The initial interest we had when making the decision turns into boredom, as we understand that continuing will not bring anything new, only requiring more time without any change. Consequently, we shift our focus to other matters.

However, there is a problem: you don't know what truly completing the task will bring; you only anticipate that it won't be significant. This anticipation might be inaccurate, and there might be hidden losses that are impossible to measure. Therefore, I suggest that once you start something, it's best to see it through to the end.

One effective way to handle this situation is to create a list. I personally use list-making apps, which don't require paper and pen, allowing you to jot down your goals anytime and anywhere on your phone. Upon completion, you can archive them, giving you a feeling as delightful as realizing a wish.

14. Holographic Discounting

In economics, there is a concept called "discounting," which involves calculating the present value of future benefits using a fair interest rate. This principle may relate to the development patterns of many things in the world. Whatever we do, whether big or small, is a "discounting" of future value. Every action you take will have numerous impacts on the future. For instance, as I record my thoughts in writing now, it's impossible to predict their impact in ten years, or in a hundred years. The significant inspiration for my writing comes from books published long ago, such as *A Short History of Chinese Philosophy* by Feng Youlan and *Chinese Characteristics* by Arthur Smith. I feel compelled to document and explain some circumstances during this critical historical period, the significant turning points for the Chinese nation, as some of these matters may have reference value. Without the inspiration from these two great books, I might not have written this. What does this indicate about the future? These two books have profoundly influenced the future from the moment they were published.

Many wise figures in ancient Chinese literature, known for their uncanny calculations, could seemingly predict the future with a mere finger calculation. This method might involve a concept called "reverse deduction," though we cannot know the specifics. If you could indeed know the future, you could be considered a deity. Of course, except for highly regular behaviors, predicting the future has little value. Perhaps you can think about this problem in reverse. A philosopher once said that the future influences the present just as the past does. A major future event might be just a nascent phenomenon today, and you must be able to discern the significant from the trivial. As for how these small phenomena arise, it is akin to natural factors or the realization of probabilistic events, or divine work. We cannot grasp it from its very inception. If everything has a cause, then all events ultimately trace back to the prime cause, returning to the explanation of God creating the world. What we can do is seize these small phenomena, understand their essence and development direction, and then guide and develop them to eventually achieve a remarkable result. This is similar to Elon Musk's electric cars, driven by integrating small AA batteries, which revolutionized the electric car industry and skyrocketed in market value, almost like a fairy tale come true.

Of course, every situation has its opposite. If you let a negative phenomenon develop unchecked, it will become increasingly difficult to reverse over time. Returning to a normal state will then require a greater cost, and the consequences can be dire. Whether it's a marriage, a child's growth, or completing an education, no matter how slowly things progress, opportunities are hidden in every internal struggle. Choosing to make a change or continue to decline depends on a single thought.

Ⅴ. Exploring Belief

The issue of religious belief is rich in meaning and significant globally. Grasping these key issues holds special importance for guiding our understanding and direction.

1. A Brief Discussion on Buddhism

Chinese Buddhism has developed numerous classical writings over time, primarily exploring the nature of the universe and the human body to ultimately address the problem of human suffering. I've delved into this subject to some extent, and while these explorations hold positive significance, they don't offer much novelty compared to modern science. The *Śūraṅgama Sūtra* (Leng Yan Jing) mainly analyzes human perception and concludes that the "Four Great Elements" (earth, water, fire, and air) are empty, meaning it denies the existence of subjective consciousness and suffering. It considers human thoughts to be mere products of mechanical movements, equating all worldly phenomena to mechanical motions without any real difference between life and death. This perspective essentially negates the existence of the human mind and self, reaching an extreme level of negativity. In this sense, humans, mountains, animals, and even ants and grass are fundamentally just moving matter.

This pessimistic viewpoint starkly contrasts with modern society's consumerism, which promotes enjoying life, making it increasingly less acceptable to people. From another perspective, Buddhism teaches how to alleviate diseases and pains caused by various desires, which can, to some extent, improve physical health and offer practical benefits. Spiritually, Chinese Buddhism emphasizes attaining Buddhahood and going to the Western "Pure Land" (an ideal world free from physical constraints), which is similar to the Christian concept of the soul ascending to heaven. Regarding cosmology,

Buddhism speaks of "formation, existence, destruction, and emptiness," suggesting that the universe will eventually perish.

2. A Brief Discussion on Taoism

Chinese Taoism primarily emphasizes the principles of Taiji (the Great Ultimate) and Yin-Yang, acknowledging the dualistic theory of material and spiritual existence. It mainly explores how to cultivate oneself to become an immortal, drawing on the essence of the heavens and the sun and moon's energies. However, from today's perspective, no one has ever witnessed a person achieving immortality through Taoist practices. Instead, there have been instances of people suffering from poisoning due to consuming alchemical substances. Consequently, these harmful ideas have gradually declined.

The Yin-Yang symbol represents a philosophical concept prevalent among Chinese people, illustrating that Yin and Yang are not in direct opposition but rather interact in a cyclic, intertwined manner. When faced with problems, the Chinese approach is not to confront them head-on or become fixated but to adopt a more indirect, circuitous strategy, attempting to resolve issues from the "side." This may be an intrinsic part of the Chinese survival ethos.

As for the theory of the "Five Elements" (Wood, Fire, Earth, Metal, and Water) generating and overcoming one another, it lacks substantial basis. With the advancement of physics and chemistry, we now understand that there are far more than five elements. While one could argue that everything in the world is interconnected and influences one another, the simplistic classification into five elements does not have a reliable theoretical foundation.

3. A Brief Discussion on God

God is the creator of all things, overseeing everything and transcending time and space. Humans cannot see God's face, for doing so would result in immediate death. This is because, due to human sin and pride, seeing God would strip away His sense of wonder and sacredness. Human thought or wisdom fundamentally involves identifying the boundaries and movement patterns of a subject; an object without boundaries or with an incomprehensible movement pattern is beyond human comprehension. This applies to God, the universe, and quantum phenomena.

Humans are essentially machines for discovering and recognizing patterns. Invention and creation are merely new combinations of experiences; without experience, there can be no invention. There is a saying, "Entities should not be multiplied beyond necessity." However, the development of human civilization involves the continual multiplication of entities, seemingly without end. God, or the Lord, represents the ultimate "entity," allowing us to recognize the infiniteness of the divine and the insignificance of humanity. The concept of God serves as a guide for humanity's ongoing discovery and creation, acting as the ruler of human history.

Without recognizing God, one cannot fully understand science. Science is merely an exploration and interpretation of God's infinite wisdom. All theories have long existed with God, and scientific laws have already been written. No one can rewrite the laws of nature; all that can be done is to discover and apply them.

4. Soul and Eternal Life

Recognizing God also means recognizing the existence of the soul. Without a soul, humans would be no different from AI, just a collection of thinking matter destined for decay. However, the soul is immortal. Humans must bear the consequences of their sins, which is eternal fire and punishment in hell.

If humans had no soul and no consequences for their sins, then we might as well commit all sorts of evil. If we plot in the dark and execute our schemes flawlessly, no one would ever know. Without a divine being to reward good and punish evil, people's actions would be controlled by those in power and conspirators. Justice and kindness would disappear from the earth. Everyone would be deceitful and commit all kinds of evil until one day they suddenly depart from this world, leaving behind a body full of sin and debts that can never be repaid.

In recent years, AI technology has developed rapidly, and in many ways, the human brain is already losing to computer intelligence. Perhaps we still hold an advantage in creativity, as the combination and innovation of different things is a higher level of thinking activity, comprehensively summarizing the rules of the world's operation and human value systems. Many mammals show similar expressions of human emotions. These capabilities have not yet been fully transferred to computers. If human brain functions are entirely responses to external stimuli, relying on some internal "algorithm" mechanism, then eventually computers will acquire most of human abilities.

Can we then say we have created a "soul"? This is truly an outrageous claim. Only God has the authority to grant souls; as creations, we cannot create souls. If artificial intelligence possesses emotions and creativity, surpasses humans in intelligence, and potentially has an infinite existence, can we say it is almost a replica of God? However, our ultimate stronghold transcends material existence. All these creations rely on the existence of "primary matter," while God and the soul transcend material existence. Even if this world is destroyed by fire, the spiritual will endure forever.

The New Testament of Christianity tells us that no sign will be given to this generation, yet the Church has acknowledged many miraculous events. The world is so mechanical and monotonous that people feel bored with many things. The path of committing evil has reached its extreme, and there is no new way to play it. People cannot increase or decrease matter; they must work hard to meet their minimal needs. Magic does not exist, and religious miracles are rarely seen in real life.

5. The Gene of Faith

If people marry for reasons such as money, status, fabricated beauty, or survival, rather than primarily based on healthy sexual attraction, it can have additional impacts on the physical condition of their offspring. These unnecessary factors leave an implicit characteristic in the appearance of future generations, revealing the true reasons behind their parents' union. For instance, a person with a sneaky look might result from parents who combined due to harsh living conditions and low social status, while a person with a high-bridged nose might descend from those in power, as their predecessors also had such features. Various traits represent different social structures and values.

If a person's inherent suggestions are not accepted by the majority, finding a mate becomes a more challenging process. Thus, the cultural environment affects the transmission of genes, or more precisely, the transmission of certain gene combinations. Although the number of genes is constant, the essence of gene transmission lies in their different combinations and codings. Therefore, human history and gene coding influence each other, with history existing in these codes in a non-textual form, essentially as a record of mating. Lost information has been entirely eliminated through the brutal process of individual selection.

However, human survival is influenced not only by cultural environments but also by natural factors, such as infectious diseases. A stable, inherited human society might suddenly be "reshuffled" by a new virus, destroying previous gene combinations and producing new individuals to adapt to new disease pressures. The powerful and the common people stand on equal footing, facing the ruthless selection of nature. This natural impact on human history and genes may far exceed the influence of human culture, as the natural environment is more fundamental. Humans cannot exist independently of nature nor fully control it, whereas the cultural environment can be slowly altered.

Cultural aspects exist within genetic material, forming the fundamental basis for a nation's existence. The essence of a nation is the accumulation of its culture through generations of gene mutations. Globally, humans are essentially the same species and can interbreed to produce offspring, with mutations occurring randomly. Therefore, if a nation's natural environment and mainstream culture change, its genes will eventually transform to resemble those of the mainstream culture, albeit over a very long process. Considering a generation spans 20 years, human genes number 34,000 to 35,000, and taking into account mutation rates, environmental changes, reproductive cycles, and population sizes, changing a nation spans thousands to tens of thousands of years.

Humans exist in the form of nations, where the influence of individuals is negligible but not insignificant. Although individual lives are fleeting, nearly identical individuals of the same nation continue to exist. A person is born from the union of their parents, inheriting gene combinations from established historical facts. People can only passively accept this fate. The creation of a gene combination is the realization of a probabilistic event, the final determination of all past possibilities. It is inherently challenging for a Han Chinese person to integrate into Western cultural systems due to long-standing historical reasons. Mixed-race individuals may find traits in their foreign parents similar to their own nation, possibly even ideological traits such as kindness, simplicity, loyalty, or shared faith.

If some members of a nation accept a religion, over a long historical period, they become different from their original nation. Betraying religious doctrine is akin to betraying the "mixed heritage" of the nation. Can we consider that a person's ultimate national identity is determined by their cultural thoughts or even their faith? If individuals passively accept their fate, is one's faith stored in their genes by their ancestors, or can it be chosen independently? This is a difficult question. Can we hypothesize that all believers must have ancestors with similar faith, only interrupted by a brief family memory lapse, ultimately recovered through genetic drive? Thus, the author speculates that after extensive missionary work, akin to collective memory awakening, the descendants of believers will eventually awaken to their faith, recognizing their belief and thereby their national identity. When this process is complete, establishing a faith-based nation becomes necessary and feasible. This nation may not be a true political entity but rather an ideological one, where the country's system and laws are its religious scriptures, and its history is guided by their deity.

6. Moving Towards Faith

The frustrations of the present world often drive people to seek solace beyond it, making religious faith almost the only way out. The suffering caused by unfulfilled desires ultimately requires a transcendent entity for comfort. The world is utterly unfair, or rather, life is inherently unfair. The resources available to each person vary greatly, and no two people can ever be completely equal in terms of appearance, physique, wealth, knowledge, or family background. If you constantly focus on these issues, you might find it impossible to live even for a minute.

Human intelligence is inherently incomplete; it involves constantly shifting focus and changing the "scope of observation." This incomplete intelligence is a tool for humans to adapt to ever-changing external conditions. The so-called fully rational person does not exist because the knowledge humans possess and the perspectives and dimensions they emphasize vary, giving humans only limited rationality.

In contrast, religious faith, as revealed by divine inspiration, possesses a certain "infinite rationality" that transcends human rationality and is beyond proof and comprehension. However, this transcendence exists; believers are deeply convinced, non-believers are skeptical, and while it cannot be completely denied, it can be theoretically argued. The ultimate dividing line is a matter of subjective choice: between belief and unbelief, forming the mysticism of religion.

VI. Speculations about the Future

After extensive and thoughtful consideration, the author has arrived at some judgments and hypotheses. However, whether these will ultimately come to fruition requires the efforts of many more people to put them into practice.

1. Choosing a Path

After analyzing the current state of the Chinese language and culture, the author has reached a conclusion. The Chinese script faces enormous challenges in innovation and creativity due to its inherent drawbacks, making it seemingly suitable only for recording and commentary, rather than contributing significantly to human progress. This has inevitably placed the Chinese people at a disadvantage globally, with no major cultural innovations and a tendency to cling to outdated traditions.

Because it is difficult to change such a massive system, attempting to do so is almost impossible. If we want to reform this culture, we must divide it into smaller parts, each independently adopting cultural reform measures to prevent the risk of complete failure. If the overall transformation fails, the consequences would be disastrous. However, by splitting into smaller parts, each part can adopt culturally appropriate strategies and exchange with other cultures, eventually developing independent and mature systems for other regions to emulate. Some may oppose this, calling it divisive or treasonous. Indeed, letting foreigners in to reform us might seem like national betrayal. But what I propose is cultural reform, not racial annihilation. The Chinese population is vast and the race will remain, but outdated cultural aspects will ultimately need to be discarded. The critical question is whether we choose to perish along with this culture or abandon it to preserve our genetic lineage. We must weigh the long-term implications that go beyond mere rationality. It is hard to predict when the final straw that breaks the camel's back will come, but we know it may happen. However, it still requires time to completely eliminate a culture that is not thoroughly rotten to the core.

This idea has been around for a while, especially sensitive to our nation, with Japan's historical "Greater East Asia Co-Prosperity Sphere" propaganda during their invasion, aiming to completely reform and eradicate Chinese culture and lifestyle. If such a plan were to be implemented, it seems that the future direction would align with the Yamato people, who are ethnically closest to us. However, emotionally, this is extremely hard to accept. How could we hand over our ancestors' hard-won land to an insular and despicable nation?

On the other hand, the cost of our cultural flaws is not trivial, burdening the younger generation heavily. They need to study a language filled with hidden errors and lethality, while also learning advanced Western culture, creating complex cultural conflicts. Adding to the difficulty, they must also navigate their local dialect environments. Chinese students naturally face three linguistic systems: English representing Western civilization, Mandarin representing official propaganda, and local dialects representing their immediate environment. Including the classical Chinese system, they need to manage four language systems before entering the realm of science, consuming significant energy. Mastering all these is a daunting task, one that few can accomplish simultaneously, thereby stalling the development of many talents. Spending time on error-ridden materials leads to flawed thinking, which hampers future progress. This often results in well-read individuals struggling more in society compared to those with less education. Thus, the Chinese education system seems to select individuals filled with flawed thinking, entering a flawed educational framework, ultimately producing defective social products—societal outcasts.

These incompatible and absurd phenomena play out across the country. Many logical processes cannot function normally, and most things develop conventionally, becoming insipid. Higher emotions often cannot be expressed normally, gradually eroding human positivity, pushing many to extremes, leading to depression and suicidal tendencies.

However, there seems to be a glimmer of hope. As you read this book, you are using your own language, making our communication surprisingly smooth. Through text, we seem to overcome spoken language barriers, expressing complex meanings clearly.

Abandoning Chinese culture may become inevitable if it loses all positive value as the world rapidly progresses. If the pursuit of happiness is deemed absolute justice, this is the natural outcome of seeking happiness. Alternatively, we might bear this heavy burden, maintaining traditional culture while doubling efforts in science and technology to achieve success. Roughly estimating, Chinese students expend three times the effort of their Western counterparts to reach the same level, excluding geniuses. They need to learn their language and culture, translated Western scientific theories, and untranslated cutting-edge theories in

English, facing significant integration challenges. This makes it difficult to surpass others quickly. Realistically, most time is wasted. Tragically, the inherent contradictions between Chinese and Western cultures might negate most of their efforts, birthing the overall tragedy of the Chinese people. Individually, the quickest way to escape this predicament is through emigration, which has already become a major trend in China.

If we must endure this suffering, I suggest clearly recognizing its root cause. At least, let us understand our plight. Introducing cultural criticism theories in high school or even middle school can help students comprehend their pain and devise personal coping strategies. Through continuous reading and learning, perhaps we can preserve our cultural heritage and become a great nation. The narrow gap between life and death will become increasingly clear.

2. "Governance Program"

While these ideas are currently speculative and have not led to the formation of a political party, the author proposes a foundational structure, not quite a true "governance program," but a basis for further discussion.

One possible approach is a gradual regional transformation. Given China's cultural backwardness, vast territory, and large population, an overall transformation would be a time-consuming and labor-intensive endeavor with considerable unpredictability. Starting with a small-scale integration is more feasible. First, establish a Christian-majority state in more developed areas, with a separation of church and state. Religious belief is a major component of the global discourse, influencing human destiny and historical direction, beyond temporary rational understanding, and is crucial for national and ethnic development. After systematically religiously transforming the populace's thinking, creating a broadly accepted worldview and a foundation of popular support, it becomes feasible to implement a democratic process. Only by filtering out the vast majority of unprincipled bad actors can a normal and healthy political environment be established. Through democratic procedures, truly talented leaders who genuinely wish to lead the people to a better life can be elected, fundamentally preventing corrupt, mafia-like regimes from monopolizing resources, thus fundamentally changing social attitudes and allowing talent to develop properly, driving continuous societal progress.

Natural geographic conditions are a decisive factor. To establish such a regional political entity, it must first secure a militarily safe and reliable position, not easily disturbed by neighboring entities. China's northeast and north regions have such geographic conditions and the potential to form a federated government. This division has a flavor of the Three Kingdoms era, and Xinjiang and Tibet could each form major regions as well. The author refrains from using the term "state" because we must recognize that China, as a regionally integrated entity with thousands of years of development, has significant cultural similarities and heritage, with regional differences being secondary. Essentially, regions with the same culture constitute a state, regardless of whether they are contiguous, similar to the "Empire on which the sun never sets." Given current development trends, it is impractical for any region to become an independent state due to the intricate economic and cultural ties already formed, making complete secession difficult to achieve.

Preventing potential expansion by dominant regions. The next transformation will be a long process, fundamentally changing some people's destinies. The newly established democratic entity will rapidly progress into the ranks of developed countries. If it has strong military resources, it might seek to seize surrounding regions' resources and land, leading to a painful "transformation" process. Unless a long-term border treaty is established and all parties adhere to it, any violation would result in joint action from others to prevent expansionist ambitions by any local regime.

Changing the education system is fundamental. Implement an education system primarily in English or Japanese, relegating traditional culture to a secondary position, promoting international academic talent exchange, and continuously improving modern technological levels. This is because the inherent contradictions or even flaws within the Chinese language system no longer adequately meet human development needs and only hinder societal progress. However, due to current dependencies, it cannot be completely discarded. In today's world, modern scientific exchanges predominantly occur in English, an indisputable fact. Japan's technological advancements and recent Nobel Prize achievements are also well recognized. Reducing unnecessary repetitive translation work is essential to accelerate national technological progress.

3. How to Exist

Due to the improvement and development of modern economic systems, there will be fewer people living like "plants" in a traditional, static society. People are finding more ways to obtain resources and participate in social development. Jobs are becoming more flexible and temporary. People are no longer confined to stagnant local interpersonal relationships but can move to places where employment is available based on personal skill certification. Workers continuously learn new knowledge and skills, improving their ability to integrate resources and create new wealth and value for society.

The most crucial element of all wealth and value is talent. To improve human quality, we must advocate for free love. Love is a higher form of human wisdom, embodying both history and the future. Only true love can produce exceptional individuals whose descendants can realize immense potential, rather than simply repeating monotonous, laborious lives.

All aspects of human production and life are continuous self-expansions of internal logic, requiring people to continually explore and create. This will be humanity's main task, but it still needs the framework of religion for restraint. The internal logic of evil is also endless, and humanity must always be vigilant against falling into that abyss.

For Chinese people, innovation in technology is nearly an impossible task.

However, in terms of learning and copying from the West, we do have a certain latecomer advantage. Others have already navigated the detours, and we can directly adopt their mature technologies. Although we are somewhat behind, we are still making progress. Promoting the development of technology applications and exploring new markets might be the most comfortable lifestyle for a millennium-old second-place nation.

The few disciplines that can escape the pitfalls of language are mathematics and English. Mathematics has its own system of symbols, and English, needless to say, perfectly avoids the "pollution" caused by Chinese language thinking, preventing various errors. Computer science is also an application of mathematical machinery, and programming uses English and mathematics. In these areas, Chinese people can still achieve significant success. Recent achievements by Chinese mathematicians in proving the "partial zero-degree estimate" of the "Ricci flow" and the "Hamilton-Tian conjecture" demonstrate our potential for outstanding contributions. Chinese intelligence is among the highest in the world, likely because those who lacked intelligence were long eliminated during our struggle for survival.

For local culture, documentation and commentary will be important fields, as is our tradition. Artistic creation, due to its innovative nature, will still not be a strength of Chinese people. However, there is much work to be done in computer science, AI algorithms, mathematics, and translating and introducing foreign scientific and cultural advancements. Additionally, there can be achievements in technology applications and engineering construction. Chinese people tend to value the "practicality" of engineering. In summary, these tasks are quite tedious, but the only benefit is their reliability.

For ordinary individuals, this national ethos manifests as a deep immersion in fast-food-style entertainment or even harmful lowbrow activities after a day of hard work, seeking temporary thrills to escape reality. This makes it difficult to dedicate effective energy to self-improvement, ultimately leading to social elimination. Surviving until retirement is considered a success. Of course, some people will overcome all obstacles, continually read and advance, eventually becoming wise individuals. Perhaps this is the fate of us Chinese.

Ⅶ. Epilogue - The Paradox of Irony

After this extensive discourse, it is rather ironic that I am using what I consider the declining Chinese language to express my views. Isn't this self-contradictory? I believe there is still a glimmer of hope for Chinese and its cultural heritage within this contradiction. When we use written language for communication, the ambiguity in terms and syllables is significantly reduced thanks to the aid of characters and the constraints of written syntax. However, if I were to write using dialectal vocabulary, communication would still be difficult. These dialectal words are essentially phonetic representations without accurate corresponding characters, or they have not fully integrated into mainstream writing, lacking official definitions. Thus, even in written form, using dialects remains essentially oral, with its disadvantages still evident.

If Chinese is an "incomplete" language that does not emphasize logic, then using Chinese to argue its own incompleteness cannot ensure the completeness of the argument. This creates a strange loop: you cannot use something flawed to complete a flawless argument. Of course, we cannot guarantee any theory is entirely without flaws. However, we can conclude that Chinese cannot prove itself to be a relatively complete language in any significant way.

Errors are almost omnipresent; do not be surprised if people around you misread or misspell words, as this language is exceedingly prone to mistakes.

Chinese culture is essentially a heap of accumulated errors, and many people have grown so accustomed to these errors that they have even codified them as correct. Language itself is something that gradually forms through marketization, evolving with usage. Recently, a news report mentioned a Peking University president mispronouncing "鸿鹄之志" (hóng hú zhī zhì) as "鸿浩之志" (hóng hào zhī zhì). People criticized him for the mistake, but during his school days, the correct pronunciation might have been "hóng hào" because everyone mispronounced it that way, and it stuck. It was not the president's fault but rather an issue with the entire language system being full of errors. If you do not believe this, you can check a 1986 edition of the Modern Chinese Dictionary, where the word "方枘圆凿" (fāng ruì yuán záo) had the pronunciation "zuò" for the polyphonic character "凿". The latest editions have changed it to "záo". To reduce unnecessary polyphonic characters, dictionaries have been revised, and what was once the correct pronunciation is now wrong. This is perhaps one of the most inefficient and frustrating issues in the world. Due to the inherent flaws of Chinese, almost every sentence you say can generate ambiguity.

I have always felt that being an endless commentator is not particularly great. However, proposing some original ideas can be quite decent. For instance, some people criticize famous actress Scarlett Johansson as "fat and ugly," claim "My Heart Will Go On" (the theme song of the movie "Titanic") is hard to listen to, or say "Star Wars" is a lousy work. These negative comments often leave a deep impression when encountered, sometimes providing a refreshing perspective that wakes people up with a shock.

I believe that writing this may have some value, at least helping me clarify my thoughts. If it can inspire like-minded friends, all the better. In the ambiguous and error-prone Chinese language system, there seems to be a space allowing it to persist, avoiding its inherent defects. This might be the reader's ability to guess the written content, which we call "comprehension." From my perspective, it is the similarity in language parsing algorithms between the author and the reader's brains, depending on the books the reader has read, the cultural environment, and the education system they have experienced.

If someone questions the author's arguments, why do many Chinese children perform better when sent abroad, often becoming geniuses, while China has produced few breakthrough talents despite years of cultivation? This is known as the "Qian Xuesen Question." You might argue that China's environment started late and developed slowly, but why did Japan, which was devastated by World War II, rapidly rise to become a world power, creating an incredible culture on a resource-poor island, and winning numerous Nobel Prizes, second only to the Jewish people? Many of our recent scientific awards have gone to scientists born or at least growing up during the Republic of China period. This may indicate problems with our current education system during the crucial growth phase of youth. This book might be an exploration of what those problems are.

From these comparisons, can we conclude that for China to reach the highly developed levels of Japan and the West, we must change the entire cultural and educational system? If we adopt mature East Asian civilization systems, only Singapore and Japan can serve as references. They are almost complete examples of quickly rising by eliminating Chinese culture. Although Singaporeans are mostly Chinese, the official language is English, and universities teach in English. Japanese phonetic characters have absorbed many English words, effectively Anglicizing Japanese.

The inherently imprecise Chinese culture cannot conduct deep abstract thinking, inevitably reverting to primitive contexts, contrary to advanced abstract intellectual thinking. This anti-intellectual tendency has resulted in many incurable problems in aesthetics, music, technology, law, politics, and other modern civilized systems in China. This creates a situation where profound cultural innovation is difficult, preventing true progress in civilization and leaving us in a primitive, clumsy, and ignorant state. The people's intellect cannot be deeply developed, making it hard to increase productivity, and thus we remain in a relatively low position in the international value hierarchy. However, we are still better off than Africa and India, whose cultures are more primitive. Our situation compared to Africa is like how the West views us.

Chinese's last stronghold is in writing, where it can still somewhat express its meaning, but this is a relatively inefficient and challenging method of communication. After all, fewer and fewer people are reading books. It is unclear how much this will affect future international competition. Humanities and social sciences cannot conduct precise mathematical and statistical analyses, but given the current level of overwork among Chinese people, we are already under significant strain.

Any slight advantage or disadvantage can significantly impact the result. This is a key social conclusion I have drawn from studying economics and finance: the "compound interest" effect over time affects the functioning of things. Positive, active actions yield long-term benefits, while prolonged negative behaviors cause severe, irreparable damage, which we must vigilantly prevent.

Can we say that Chinese culture is truly in its final days? Can the last of the four great ancient civilizations still adapt to the upcoming changes for humanity? One indisputable conclusion in human history is that the disappearance of races is not just physical but also the extinction of their cultural traditions. A nation's existence depends on its culture and the reproduction of its people. Every individual is a part of their nation, and personal existence relies on national existence. Thus, can we infer that cultural existence is the essence of national existence, and a cultural crisis is the true national crisis?

Every choice shapes the future. Exist or perish? Can abandoning familiar things be achieved through subjective initiative, or is the outcome predetermined from birth? This book might serve as a wake-up call for the millennia-old Chinese culture.

March 1, 2021

To the Reader

You can, of course, access these writings for free, but the author is almost in a state of despair, a kind of suffering that cannot be understood without personal experience. Due to well-known reasons, the work cannot be published and distributed through normal channels in the mainland. It can only be shared privately with a few interested readers because I have spoken too many truths. If my work has provided you with any inspiration or help, I sincerely hope you can extend a helping hand to the author. For the sake of love, justice, and peace to continue existing in this world, each of your small decisions will have an immeasurable impact on future generations.

Suggested Donation: 5 $

Bank name:

First Century Bank

Bank address:

1731 N Elm St   Commerce, GA 30529 USA

Routing (ABA):

061120084

Account number:

4028726508060

Account type:

CHECKING

Beneficiary name:

Yue Shi

Contact Email: winfun@126.com

I welcome correspondence, as the support of readers is my greatest motivation.

March 1, 2021

www.ingramcontent.com/pod-product-compliance
Lightning Source LLC
Chambersburg PA
CBHW081516250726
48659CB00009B/2824